DON'T ABDICATE THE THRONE

Why And How Women Should Find Their Power,
Crash Their Own Party,
And Take Control Of Their Lives

Lisa Brooks-Greaux, ED.D.

Printed in the United States of America

First Printing, 2019

ISBN: 978-1-73350-250-4 (print)
ISBN: 978-1-54396-042-6 (ebook)

Copyedited by: Kirkus Reviews
Proofread by: Linsey Doering of Dot and Cross Creative Services
Published in the United States by: BookBaby

Mom, you were always ahead of your time.
This one's for you.

CONTENTS

PREFACE

Time to Get Uncomfortable

LET ME ASK YOU A FEW QUESTIONS: HOW DO YOU SEE yourself? What does the ultimate you look like? What about your voice? Have you discovered it? What do you want out of life? And are you in control of it?

My name is Lisa Brooks-Greaux. Born to working-class parents and raised in the Pocono Mountains of rural Pennsylvania, I had no special advantages as a child to suggest that I would go on to enjoy a full and multifaceted life. By the grace of God, however, I did. I found my path to the Fortune 100 and Fortune 500 arenas where I twice served in the capacity of vice president. Through the nod of corporate accolades, I've been afforded the humbling confirmation that my contributions have been deemed, at least in the eyes of some, helpful. I have enjoyed the privilege of being invited by different groups to speak about my work, including the Global Human Resources Forum in Seoul, Korea, where I was a keynote speaker. I've had the honor of working as the executive sponsor of a company's women's council and seeing that company named a top ten place of business for working mothers. I've had the good fortune of extensive travel, both domestically and overseas, and establishing lifelong connections with friends and colleagues spanning the globe. I've experienced the joy of mentoring and of blossoming under the guidance of mentors and coaches whom I can only describe as angels on Earth. But all this would be a mere dish without seasoning were it not for the most important ingredients that have brought true richness to my life: a loving life partner, supportive family, loyal friends, good health, and, most importantly, an unwavering faith in God. My spiritual guidance has been, without question, my North Star.

I come to you here as an everyday woman. I have worn the hats of daughter, sister, aunt, friend, wife, mentor, educator, human resources executive, coach, keen people observer, and even wannabe hip-hop dancer. Driven by a love of drawing out the natural-born strengths we all have, I have treasured each role. Above all else, however, I am a quiet disrupter. I am the one who will poke holes in the status quo, ask how you could rework the equation to solve a problem or tweak the script so that it fits your goals. After all, you want to make something truly wonderful of your life. You want to feel that sense of purpose, don't you?

My first steps in the world of strength development came when I was still a toddler holding my mother's hand. Like most children, I walked around on my stubby little legs with an intense curiosity about the world and the people around me. I was that three-year-old who pummeled her parents—particularly her mother—with the recurring tape of the top FAQs by toddlers: "How does this work, Mommy?" "What's that?" "Who is that person over there?" Naturally, I'd respond to most answers she gave me with a "Why?"

On and on I'd go.

But God blessed me with an exceptional mother.

Each time I consulted my companion encyclopedia, she'd smile down at me and answer with patience and thoughtfulness. In fact, I can't remember her ever cutting me off, feeding me a cookie-cutter reply, or showing exasperation. Like I said, she was no ordinary woman. A few years later, at about the time when I was learning to tie my own shoelaces, my mother changed the game on me *for* me.

Now after answering my questions, she would add one or two of her own: "So what do you think that means, Lisa Anne?" "What would you do if you were that person?" "What do you think about this . . . or that?" She would tease my thoughts out of me as if it were perfectly natural to seek the perspective of a six-year-old kid. As if saying it for the first time every time, she would praise me for the brilliant questions I asked, tell me how smart I was, and insist that I could be anything I wanted in this world.

All I had to do was believe it.

And I believed her just as I knew sugar was sweet.

I couldn't have seen it then, of course, but she was raising her daughter to have an opinion of her own—a point of view. She was showing her not only how to express her views but also that it was OK to have them even if they contradicted someone else's. By focusing on intelligence, character, and personality, the woman who gave me life gave me my voice. She made it clear that I was in charge of my world and that I reigned over my kingdom.

Naturally, the six-year-old Lisa thought the whole question-and-answer exercise was pretty lame. She also assumed that all parents talked to their kids this way. She was wrong, of course.

About fifteen years later, Mom revealed the reason behind those structured interactions.

We were out doing some light shopping one Saturday afternoon when a woman in a sharp outfit walked by. She was attractive, not just in her facial features but in the way she was put together and moved. By her steady, self-assured gait, her head pointed ahead of her with shoulders squared, you knew she was aware of the striking image she cut.

But that wasn't all that won my attention.

There was a certain air about her. A sense of sweet anticipation that suggested she was about to enjoy something wonderful. It was as if she were sitting in an exquisite white tablecloth restaurant and the most sumptuous, perfectly plated dish had just been placed before her.

I stared more than I should have, almost to the point of being rude, and then commented to my mother on how stunning the lady was. After giving the passerby a quick glance, my mother replied with a perfunctory, almost unimpressed, "Oh, yes, I suppose she is."

It occurred to me only then that my mother had never commented on people's looks or, for that matter, anything that involved anyone's outward appearances. Including mine. I wanted to know why.

So I did what she taught me. I asked.

"Mom," I said, "when I was little, did you not think I was pretty?"

She looked at me with a small start while we continued our leisurely stroll.

"Gosh, of course I did. You were my beautiful little girl. But surely you knew that. I told you, didn't I?"

"Well, no," I replied with a wry smile. "Not really. Not *ever*, actually. Why was that?"

Her cover blown, she gave me a solemn nod.

"No question about it, baby girl, I thought you were beautiful. Everyone did. And just look at you now. You're nothing short of gorgeous."

I smiled, happy to be sharing this moment with my mom. We always had a good time together. If we weren't mother and daughter, we'd be friends.

"But you never said anything because . . . ?"

This time she barely paused before giving me a mother-knows-best smile.

"Because I wanted you to develop something that would last forever—character. I didn't want you to take the easy way out and focus on your outer beauty. Your looks are a blessing, yes, but they will fade with age. I know this because it happens to everyone. *Everyone.* But character and intellect, now those only improve with time. That's why I made my children focus on books over looks. I wanted them to learn how to carry out actual conversations. I wanted them to use their brains. *Especially* my daughter."

Then she stopped walking and turned her petite five-foot-one frame toward me.

"Lisa Anne, the most dangerous thing in this world is a woman who can think for herself. Never forget that."

Years later, in a conversation with my brother, Joey, I learned that Mom did not exactly put him through the same training camp as she did me. At first I was surprised. But then the old adage came to mind: "Mothers raise their daughters but love their sons."

At that moment I understood that my wise mother had known all along what she was preparing me for: life as a woman in what is often a man's world. For the benefit of my (younger) female readers, I want to point out that while this seems unfair at first blush, it is actually a show of an even deeper love.

Why? It takes more out of parents to intervene and actively nurture their children than to leave it to nature to take its course, especially when it means possibly being at odds with them for even a short period.

Only decades later would I realize that my mother was both brilliant and ahead of her time.

The revelation came one day while talking with a friend who, for all her intelligence, strength, and grace, was grappling with self-doubt. Some ten years my junior, Nadia was like a little sister to me. Determined, hardworking, and always ready with a quick smile, the forty-year-old mother of four had made it her mission to give her children the life and opportunities she never had. A popular and much-loved individual in her church and community, she was also the ultimate wife, daughter, friend, and human being.

But on that day, the normally feisty beauty with the dewy brown skin and piercing eyes to match greeted me with what felt like a manufactured smile. Despite her fairly convincing act called "I'm fine, thanks," a performance we women generally excel at, I sensed that Nadia was feeling down. It was the kind of haunting frustration that only another woman's radar can detect beneath the vinyl of a perky voice and careful selection from the thesaurus of upbeat words. You know you're doing your best. You know you're needed. You even know you're loved. And yet you're just a little overwhelmed by a life of service that feels all too underacknowledged. I listened as she tried to hide the hurt with humor.

When she finally paused to muster a brave smile, I shook my head and told her how she appeared to me. I told her that I saw this incredible woman who showed up every day for her children, instilling confidence in them, organizing their schedules, and molding their beautiful, young minds. But before I could continue, she burst into tears. Thinking that I had misread her and upset her further, I immediately began to apologize.

"No, no," she said, drying her eyes with the back of her hand and adding an embarrassed laugh. "It's just that no one has ever said they see me this way—or see me at all."

I stood there in silence, playing back her words in my mind.

It was then that I understood what a rare gift my mother and father had given me. In that moment, I got a glimpse of what the other Lisa might have looked like had she been born into a different family. I imagined being an impressionable young girl with parents who, while filled with love for their daughter, could not dream big enough for her because they didn't know how to, and who didn't understand that a child's radar picks up on such signals. And I imagined being a young woman going through life with a partner who sometimes forgot the importance of validation.

Honestly, this new insight unnerved me. In that moment, my "why" for this book was born.

The final impetus to write it came one Saturday afternoon while in my neighborhood Borders between the shelves of the business section.

A voracious reader, I was happiest when hunkered down in that bookstore for hours, sitting on the floor or in a chair with a new treasure and leaving with four or five new purchases. My passion was, and still is, talent development and leadership. On that particular day, I had gone in search of women's perspectives on the topic.

Without even trying, I immediately found titles written by men, for men. Hopeful, I kept digging. In the end, the bookshelves offered only a few titles on leadership written by female authors and even fewer by women of color. This gave me a much-needed jolt to the system as a small kernel of resentment lodged itself in my throat.

I knew of so many outstanding women who were brilliant leaders—women who had overcome major obstacles to achieve their end goals. So where were their books? Why were they not represented here? Why were we not hearing their voices and words of advice? Why was half the workforce not being properly represented?

While I had always wanted to pursue my doctorate, I knew at that moment that I wanted to take it further. Then and there, I made it my mission to add to the body of literature about women and leadership. Our stories are just as valuable as men's. Our stories deserve to be on bookshelves, too.

Don't Abdicate the Throne is a rallying cry for women to take control of our lives instead of relinquishing power in the many ways we sometimes do, big and small. The throne, of course, speaks to the position of power that we have over our world. While it is our right to sit in this leadership role, we can lose it if we're not careful. Whether we want to admit it or not, each time we stop pushing ourselves because we get scared, we're giving up the opportunity to determine our destiny. We stop trying because it's getting too hard, or because we don't want to be responsible for our own decisions, or because we fear failure. And while it's true that women are nurturers and tend to sacrifice for the sake of others—often out of necessity—I have also seen cases where women deliberately redirect every ounce of their energy toward their husband or children in order to avoid addressing their own hopes and aspirations. Let's face it. It's easier to cheer someone from the sidelines than to step into the arena. It's simpler to play victim and blame someone else when things don't quite work out for us. It's much more comfortable playing it safe or small. But how rewarding is it?

More than a confidence boost or show of support, this book walks you through some of the more practical steps you can take toward a leadership role, whether it be in your home, in a corporation, in a volunteer organization, or in a company of one. Leadership, after all, is about taking charge and sailing in the direction of a specific destination. And when it comes to her life, a woman should always strive to lead her ship.

Using some of my own missteps and strides as examples, I'll set out some of the questions you should be asking yourself at the various stages of your own life and point out some of the experiences you want to collect along the way. While it's true that life can be more meandering than linear, there are still decisions you can make at each milestone and in each situation that will serve you well over time.

I'll talk about asking for what you want or need in order to move ahead, finding a mentor, embracing healthy risks, taking stock of your skills, knowing who you are, getting the right kind of exposure and experience, and recognizing the benefits of failure. And I'll talk about taking the rules that have been written mainly by men, for men, and making them work for us, even if means tweaking them a little—or a lot.

Who should read this book?

Admittedly, much of my advice benefits the new college graduate or the younger woman still in the nascent stages of her career. You've established the fact that you have some ambition. You earned that degree and maybe even secured that elusive internship. You know how to think critically. You have something to share and contribute. You want to be successful, but you're not sure you can, or want to, play by the traditional rules. And by "rules," I'm referring to the societal blueprint established over a hundred years ago during the rise of the corporate world, which typically saw the man taking the stage as the lead character in the workplace and the woman in the supporting role, raising their children and taking care of the home. And while women deviated from these rules even back then, such pioneering attempts were, and still are, penalized, whether subtly or not. At the very least, playing by the traditional rules robs women of the unique gifts and strengths that we have to offer.

But despite the climb ahead, you still want in. You still want to forge ahead and rewrite that playbook. You're standing there asking, *Now what?*

- Do I want a profession?

- Do I want to go the corporate route?

- What about working for a nonprofit organization?

- What should my next move be?

- How do I get the right experience?

- How do I form relationships in the workplace?

- Should I get a mentor? How do I go about doing that?

- What kinds of questions should I be asking when I'm twenty-two if I want to be a CEO at forty-two? And what kinds of experiences should I be seeking if that's my goal?

I admit that to some extent I am writing this book to my younger self.

Had someone handed me a guide like this at my college graduation, I am quite certain I would have made it even higher up the corporate ladder than I did. But with no such playbook or guide to go by, I didn't know how to leverage my strengths. I didn't even know what that looked like, to be honest. Nor did I understand the first thing about navigating the political front line of a company. But that's just the start.

It didn't occur to me then that I should be asking myself important questions periodically. I didn't see that I needed to look back at the end of each month or week and analyze what had transpired. I didn't know that I needed to ask myself questions that would encourage personal growth:

- What am I not paying enough attention to?

- What do I need to work on?

- How do I learn best?

- How do I grow from here?

- What should my next step be?

None of these questions came to me because I wasn't thinking or acting like a leader. In fact, the idea of one day being a CEO completely escaped my radar because I didn't even see it as a possibility. I didn't have the awareness that ambition was something I could embrace. It was a language I didn't know existed.

Even worse, I neglected to ask myself questions regarding my personal life. As women, like it or not, we do have to think about a family in the context of our careers, or vice versa. Do you want marriage? What about children? Yes? No? Not sure? Have you even thought about it?

No one told me in plain words that I needed some kind of life plan. No one suggested that, at twenty-one, I needed to look beyond graduation and that first job and at least give some cursory thought to these things. That kind of purposeful focus finally snapped into place when I was in my late thirties. By then it was just a little late for me to complete the blueprint that I didn't even know I had, buried somewhere inside me.

While it is the younger generation that will benefit most from this book, I have not forgotten those of us past this stage. In the chapter on reinventing yourself, for instance, I speak to the most vulnerable among us: the women who sacrificed their careers and independence for their families, perhaps never planning to return to work, who discover one day that they either want to or have to go back to work. They are part of this conversation, too. These are our sisters who got swept up in wave after wave of messages that suggested we wait for our Prince Charming to rescue us before disappearing with him into the sunset to help build his dreams.

I am by no means suggesting that there is anything wrong with this path, merely that there are others we can take. At times, I, too, felt the pull of that powerful current. I was intrigued by the idea of being swept off my feet and "rescued." But that changed when I bought my first home—by myself—at the age of twenty-eight. That's when I realized that I didn't have to delay my plans or happiness until I found my partner. I didn't have to wait until I found "the one" to buy nice furniture. I didn't have to settle for a mattress on the floor. No. I could get a nice bed, a frame, and even a headboard.

As for the men in the audience, a good chunk of the advice may resonate with you, too. Feel free to apply it to your own journey. At the very least, this book will help you understand what your wives, daughters, sisters, or girlfriends go through in the workplace, the factors we must consider as we shape our lives, and the hurdles we must overcome to ensure a secure future. Perhaps by understanding our journey a bit more, you will feel better prepared to join in the ongoing dialogue about creating a workplace and social construct that is more balanced.

Closest to my heart, however, is what readers will encounter again and again as they turn these pages.

In an era in which good news rarely makes the headlines, you'll hear refreshing, heartwarming stories about women hoisting other women up and along or, in some cases, women pushing each other across the finish line in the true spirit of sisterhood—with no expectation of reciprocity. These are the not-so-sexy examples of women being communicative instead of competitive with one another, the kind of camaraderie that I was blessed with.

But I am not naive. I know only too well that I am among the lucky ones. For those of you who haven't been as fortunate, who were subject to the destructive mean-girls culture perpetuated through today's popular reality shows, I feel compelled to share all I have learned and tell you that this does not have to be your reality. Like me, you can enjoy the support and warmth of a band of sisters. You just need to find them. And with some faith and patience, you will.

So here's to thinking for ourselves and putting our heads together. More importantly, here's to holding our heads up so we can keep those crowns where they belong.

Lisa

1

Pen. Paper. Plan.

("I don't want to see a single wrinkle
on my face before I'm fifty.")

GOALS.

Today's generation has dusted off that once-stiff word and repackaged it with a fresh vibe. Not that it had lost its positive connotations mind you, but the idea of reaching for a higher level in just about anything—from the superficial to the super important—has become super cool. (PS. For those of you unfamiliar with the new slang, it is used as an adjective as well as a noun, so please ignore what appear to be grammatical faux pas.)

"Mary has an awesome life. She's goals."

"You really know how to deliver a speech. You're goals!"

"That lady is pumping iron at eighty? Goals!"

No matter how you say it, making goals a part of your DNA is one of the secrets to squeezing the most out of your life. When you use it in your everyday talk, even casually, what you're really doing is tuning in to the frequency of achievement.

Lever-AGE

I take you back to January, 2017. I am a faculty member at Montclair State University. For the first time, I am teaching undergraduates— perfect molding material—sharing with these students my knowledge and experience in a business management course (Management 300-Integrated Core Management).

Watching the young faces file into the classroom on that first day, I remember what I was like at their age. (And don't get me started on how I'd kill to be that age again.) While I was not completely rudderless then, I wasn't exactly facing life with any kind of roadmap, either. I wasn't peering terribly far into the future or asking myself questions that required anything more than level one introspection. My lackluster approach had nothing to do with intelligence. I had always been a consistently strong student who made her As.

The problem was that I was making two flawed assumptions:

1. I assumed that "it" (i.e., life) would just come together for me.

2. I assumed that I had time. And lots of it.

Depending on your age and life experiences, dear reader, this confession will make you either shrug or shiver. Those in the latter group know only too well that without focus and awareness, even the most intelligent, highly talented, well-connected, and ultraprivileged individuals can still miss their mark. Planning, after all, sits upstream from success.

Back to my young guinea pigs.

"You guys are at this perfect, delicious age," I begin once they've settled down and the screeching of chairs has finally stopped. "But in ten years," I say with a snap of my fingers held high for a touch of theatrics, "you're going to be thirty. Then forty."

A collective gasp sweeps across the room, eyes widening as if I've just canceled Christmas. Because this is the reaction I'm looking for, I can't help but suppress a mischievous grin. I know they're probably assuming I'm about to follow up with some reassuring message. But I'm not handing out any candy today. Nope. Today I'm giving them the in-your-face speech I wish someone had force-fed me when I was young.

I continue.

"Think about this. Only ten years ago you were ten. You remember ten, right? Didn't that fly by?"

Heads nod as my students begin to lean forward. I have their attention now.

"You have two choices. You can live by accident, or you can live by design. I'm all for being free-spirited, but there comes a time when you need to fix your feet on the path that'll take you to your chosen destination. Time goes by regardless of what you do. It will not wait for you to be ready. You will turn thirty, God willing. And then forty.

And so on. So why not be twenty-five or thirty or forty with a couple of goals already under your belt?

"*This* is your time. You're standing at the door of this amazing event called life. Your neurons are firing like crazy. Your brain is this incredible damp sponge. Your body is filled with youthful, robust energy just waiting to be unleashed on the world. You will never be here again.

"Grab the moment. Throw your arms around it. Think about how you're going to spend your time and precious energy. Ask yourself some tough questions: Who are you? What do you want? Don't know that yet? No problem. What about the things you refuse to accept? Start there and use the process of elimination. We almost always know instinctively what our deal-breakers are. Make a plan. Yes, life will throw you some challenges, but if you have a road map for your life, you'll get back on track instead of merely drifting to the next stop and wondering twenty years from now who the person in the mirror is, and why you don't recognize them."

I let them marinate in that visual for a while.

Self-Interrogation

When I was an undergrad, I had some vague notion of getting a nice job after college and becoming a supporting cast member in my future husband's life.

I gave no real thought to the possibility of taking the lead. It never occurred to me that I should be thinking about blueprints and plans. (Isn't that for older folks?) And while one could argue that few twenty-year-olds think that way, I would argue that maybe that's because we older and wiser folks don't encourage them to nearly enough. How I wish someone had sat me down for such a conversation. How I wish I had given thought to having my very own secret cache of goals for the future.

If I could go back, this is what I would ask my twenty-year-old—no, make that eighteen-year-old self:

- What kind of lifestyle do you hope to have? Will your chosen field support it?

- What kind of company do you see yourself working for? Large? Small? Start-up?

- How far up the ladder do you want to go? Head of a division? Do you see yourself as CEO one day?

- How do you feel about entrepreneurship? Would you have the patience, perseverance, and risk tolerance it requires?

- Do you want to work overseas? For long stints or shorter jaunts?

- Do you want marriage? No? Yes? Not sure?

- What kind of mate are you looking for? (While I will leave this topic for the experts, I'd suggest you consider someone who treats you like a queen, loves your strong mind, thinks your goals are hot, and is also working toward goals of their own.)

- Do you want to have children? If so, how many? And do you have a cutoff age for having kids, whether naturally or by adoption?

- Would you prefer to be a parent who works in the home or outside of it?

Life is unpredictable. This we know. It's impossible to plan every detail. What's more, we don't always know where our passions lie, especially when we are young. And even then, our likes and dislikes can and do change with time and experience. That's normal. The point of this exercise is not so much to solve the equation this very moment but to know that it exists. You want to at least plant that awareness in the recesses of your mind.

Being able to check your proposed blueprint at intervals, regardless of where you are in life, will help to keep you focused. It will act as your "manual" when you're facing an intersection or even an opportunity that, while intriguing at first glance, may actually be an unnecessary detour in disguise. I did eventually marry, but not until I was in my late thirties—a little too late for me to have children of my own, as it turned out.

This is not to state a regret. I am married to the man meant for me and God has blessed me with many nieces and nephews to help nurture. But here's the thing: Carl and I had actually met several years before we started to date. Had I had my blueprint clear in my head at that point, I might have done a little more than take note of how cute he was. I'm just sayin'.

The Write Ritual

I developed the habit of planning by pen while in graduate school.

So hooked was I on my new ritual, I summoned my nieces and nephews the following New Year's Day to share with them this new discovery. I was not going to let "my children" wander through life without this secret weapon for success. At the time, their ages ranged from twelve to twenty-one. Even though they were secretly rolling their eyes, they obliged their Auntie Lisa and came over for our first session.

Thanks to my brother and two older half sisters (from my biological father's first marriage), there are eleven kids with whom I've had the joy of meeting like this annually at our goal-setting party. I'm proud to say that even after seven years, we have yet to lose a single member.

This is not your usual New Year's resolution–making exercise where we casually voice grand wishes. While there is some overlap with New Year's resolutions, these goals are more granular. I tell my young charges—most likely far too often, I'm sure they'd say—that had I done this at their age, I'd have been CEO of some company by now. I am that sure of it. Once the teasing subsides, we sit at my round kitchen table and get to work on this family ritual.

The instructions are simple:

1. Write your goals in the present tense, using the active (i.e., command) voice. (For example: "Save off the top monthly." "Spend two hours a week learning a second language.")

2. Keep this list somewhere highly visible so that your eyes hit it daily. (For example: by your computer, on your desk, or on your bathroom mirror.)

3. Respect the list. It will remind you of your standards and personal agreements when you've fallen off the wagon, as we all do now and then.

As we are multidimensional, I have them write their intentions with attached deadlines in seven specific categories:

1. **Physical**

   How do you view your physical health? Do you want exercise or sports in your life? Do you want to be in marathon shape? Is your goal to get to age fifty without the need for medication to control high blood pressure, cholesterol, or diabetes? Or will you happily reach for the pills when, or if, that time comes? If you prefer the former, you may want to assess your eating and exercise habits now as a preventative strategy. Do you want to preserve as much of your youthful skin as you can? Or will you march into the plastic surgeon's office after decades of sun worshipping and have them reverse the damage? If the former, you want to think about a good skincare regimen, limited sun exposure, and sensible sleep habits sooner than later. Pick up a sport or hobby you enjoy early in life. Make working out as much a part of your routine as brushing your teeth. Give these seemingly distant matters serious thought now. Your future self is counting on your present-day self to make the right choices.

2. Financial

How's your financial health? I was just ten when my biological father died of emphysema. In the few years I had him in my life, he helped set the foundation for my financial well-being, not just by being a loving parent and fierce defender of his family but also by being a good teacher.

A bartender by trade who had also worked for years as a coal miner, Hosea Brooks learned the value of money by earning it hourly. My beloved father passed on to his kids what he knew to be the foundation of financial health: spend less than you earn, save consistently, and believe in the power of compounding interest. When I was only eight, he opened savings and checking accounts for me as well as a Christmas club account. At the time, all I had on me to deposit was some birthday or Christmas money, but it didn't matter. Because of my father, I became familiar early on with the rush of balancing my checkbook, watching my savings grow, and making a budget work. Most importantly, I became familiar with the feeling of taking control of my own money. By my third deposit I was hooked.

Learn financial literacy early. Set up your accounts. Save regularly and spend wisely. Sow the seeds for a healthy credit score early in life. Don't let a bad score be the reason you can't put a deposit on a starter home at twenty-eight.

3. **Social**

What are your friends like? Do they add something to your life? I'm not talking about using people for their social status or their potential as a personal gofer. Rather, I'm asking whether or not they bring out the best in you. Do you learn from them? Do you like their habits? Are they the kind of people you would emulate? Are they working to make the most out of their talents? Or do you think you should be making better quality connections? What about your family? Do you make time for the ones you love? Do you show them how much you appreciate them?

Whom you bring into your network says a lot about how you see yourself. Make no mistake about this. Your choice of friends can have a profound effect on your future. This is especially true when you're young. If you want proof of this, just think about past schoolmates who drifted into the classic "wrong crowd." How did their lives end up? Why do you think they chose to align themselves with these individuals?

Those of us past a certain age can easily look back and see which of our friends made us raise the bar and which enabled laziness or harmful habits. This is not to say that you're easily influenced. But there is truth to the suggestion that you are the average of the five people you spend the most time with. This is one area over which you have control. Choose wisely. I once met a girl who bragged that she always ensures that she's the "dummy" in her group. I thought she was pretty smart for having such discerning standards.

4. **Spiritual**

From which well do you draw strength when life challenges you? What keeps you soldiering on? You may not see the need for it when you're young, but faith will often be the only thing you have to pull you back up when life brings you to your knees and reminds you that you're not always in charge. Such moments came early for me in life. I would not be where I am today were it not for my strong faith. This I know for sure.

Faith does not have to come from any one religion or even "religion" as we know it. It can simply be an acknowledgment that there is more to us than the flesh we see—a force or energy inside us that we can tap into when we think our tank is empty. Even though our network of family and friends is there to cheer us on, we alone are responsible for clearing the hurdles in our lane.

I know you've seen this. You may have had a friend struggle in the past with a problem. You encouraged and supported them. You took their every SOS call. But, ultimately, they had to do the work. That may be you one day. Be prepared. Make room in your life for faith.

5. **Career**

How will you make your living? Will you work for a company or be your own boss? Or both? Is there a profession, field, or trade that interests you? Fills you with purpose? Would it be able to feed, clothe, and shelter you? Would it eventually lead to financial freedom, whatever that looks like for you?

We are all blessed with some talent that makes us glow from within. Spend time ferreting out your innate skills and strengths. Think about how you can best leverage them. Challenge yourself to work harder while you're still young. Ignore the temptation to coast early. If you think it's tough now, I promise you that it will feel worse when you're older and unable to function on five hours' sleep. We all have twenty-four hours in a day. How you spend yours now will determine what rewards you reap later.

6. **Marriage**

Do you see yourself with a life partner? Or are you quite happy being the sole mate? Admittedly, this subject can be difficult if you know you want a companion.

Do we wait for the right time or the right person? What does that perfect mate even look like? What about children? Would becoming a parent be your crowning glory or runner-up wish to something else (e.g., travel, career, lifestyle)? Would you consider adoption if you couldn't have children of your own?

While medical advancement has given women a wider window of reproductive opportunity, we are still only given a window for what is often considered one of the most important decisions a woman can make. It's not fair but it's fact. As my mom used to tell me when I felt a pity party looming, "Suck it up, buttercup!"

And while we're talking about parenthood and careers, let me say that I'm not suggesting you choose one at the expense of the other. While motherhood didn't happen for me, I think that I would have tried to have both. And many women do. Some have the gift of a boss who's flexible, a partner who's willing and able to make some sacrifices, or family willing to lend a hand. If this is you, consider yourself truly blessed. Either way, it's an important decision. Be honest with yourself. State clearly what you want.

7. **Fun** (Yes, we include fun time.)

How do you establish balance in your life? It may sound ridiculous to see "fun" as a category for goals, but we can easily fall into the trap of focusing all our attention in one area to the detriment of another.

When I was in college, I studied hard but went soft on the lighter side of life. While this may have gotten me great grades, I still wish I had engaged my playful side more. Do you enjoy a dance form? Is there an artist in you? What about learning to play an instrument? Or a sport? What makes you relax and forget your woes if even for an hour? What kind of hobby would give you a sense of balance? What fuels your creative side? What helps you reset and recharge?

When life gets busy, you'll be tempted to sacrifice playtime. Resist this. The ability to mentally recharge is too important. You are too important.

The Power of Intention

The goal-setting party is not just an excuse to spend time with my crew of kids. I want their success as much I want my own.

No doubt you've heard this before, but committing to your intentions in writing is the first step to self-actualization. It is a habit that many successful people use. (And if you want to learn more, add *Write It Down, Make It Happen* by Henriette Anne Klauser to your reading list.)

To be clear, I don't let those kids get away with merely declaring their goals. No. To make it stick, we add an accountability component. Everyone understands that they have to return the following year with an update. Did you make your deadlines? If yes, super! If no, then why not? What got in the way and how can you do better? The goal, of course, is to see a beautiful line of checkmarks going down those lists. If you're not yet familiar with list making, I promise you that crossing off items or placing a fat checkmark next to them can hit addiction levels.

But don't wait for New Year's Day. Pick your day—any day. Make your list. Get busy. Act with intention and watch the magic unfold. I have done this for over twenty years now and can proudly say that most of my goals have a checkmark next to them. Do this so it becomes part of your DNA, just as making your bed is.

The Proof Is in the Wedding

When Carl and I began dating, I knew early into the relationship that he was the one. An absolute gentleman, he rescued me one night following an after-work event I had in Manhattan. By the time the event ended, public transportation had already switched to its reduced nighttime service. Desperate, I called to ask whether he could come and get me. When he made the impromptu trip with a smile even though it robbed him of three hours of sleep in the middle of the working week, I knew that this was a good man.

Things were going well. I was confident that we would end up making a life together. But then I thought, *Hm. I'll write it down anyway.* And so I wrote: "Wait for Carl to ask me to marry him." I showed it to him a few years after our wedding. "OK, that's a little scary," he said. "What else do you have on that list of yours?"

The End

Here's another strategy that successful people use: begin with the end.

Setting goals is easy. Achieving them, however, requires perseverance. Perseverance requires focus. And focus means holding a steady eye on your endgame. Whatever you call it to make it more attractive—the prize, the pot of gold, the dream—keep your eye on that finish line. Looking at obstacles along the way may trigger paralysis. Always and only keep your eye on the end goal.

Visualize it. See it.

Let that image be so compelling that it pulls you forward day after day. Elite athletes use this technique to power through the daily grind of training when their muscles are on fire and their limbs are threatening to fall off their weary bodies. They picture themselves holding up that trophy as the roar of the crowd swells and swirls through the stadium.

To get me through my dissertation, I held in mind the image of the hooding ceremony and nonstop smile that would be plastered on my face. Before writing the first sentence of this book, I penned the acknowledgments page, while down in Atlanta, my friend Stacey went scouting for book-signing venues for me. And even though it isn't an actual goal of mine, sometimes, while sitting in traffic or doing some chores, I imagine myself rocking some killer moves in a chart-topping hip-hop video. (Oh yeah, you know what I mean!) Not only does the private reverie help pass the time away, but it gives me a rush of serotonin that fuels my day.

Get busy.

- Feel your goals like they're part of your skin.

- Know that you're worthy of your dreams.

- See the prize already in your hands.

To make this early planning stage sink in deep, I encourage young people to do something a little unorthodox: talk to someone near the end of his or her life. Become acquainted with someone a couple of generations ahead of you while you're still in your youth. Find someone you admire—maybe a mature woman who's still sporting a youthful smile. Even better, find someone who once thrived (or is still thriving) in the career you've chosen for yourself. Ask them how they did it. Ask them if they would do anything differently if they had the chance to live their life over.

Then, if you're brave, find someone who seems to have fallen short of their dreams. This would be the person who represents a place or position you never want to find yourself in. Sit with them. Have some tea. Go for a walk. Ask them how they got to this place. Ask them where they took a wrong turn. Ask them how they would rewrite the chapters of their life if they could. If you've chosen wisely, you will learn more in that single conversation than in any classroom.

I treasure the advice of older folks. Their experience, insight, and wisdom are gifts. In my own survey, I learned that we need to do the following:

- *Be present.* Don't invite your past or your future to share in the moment you're having now. Ninety-five percent of life is about simply showing up.

- *Embrace imperfection.* So what if your house isn't perfectly decorated? Who cares if your garden isn't as magazine manicured as your neighbor's? So what if you're not sporting the latest trend? You won't remember most of it anyway five or fifty years from now.

- *Avoid overthinking.* One wise elder even said that we ought not to obsess too much about finding the perfect job as long as we get close enough to it. Even if you do end up choosing one that's all wrong for you, she said, you will have gained experience and confirmation about what you don't want.

- *Appreciate our age each step of the way.* Don't wait until you're sixty to admire how you looked at thirty. Celebrate the beautiful woman you are right now.

- *Find some form of passive income.* Your energy *will* wane as you get older, even if you're in perfect health. You *will* get to the point where you won't be able to swap time for money. Plan for that stage of your life.

- *Reach for your dreams.* "I wish" remain the words most spoken by those at the end of their life, and the regret usually involves something the speaker did *not* do. I don't know of a phrase more laden with sadness than this. We feel it the moment we hear it. The speaker's gaze lowers, her shoulders slump, and her voice falls away. The air around her grows heavy. You can almost feel the emptiness she's tried to live with. Regret is poison. Make it your mission to stay clear of it.

Ready?

If you're still in your teens, you may be thinking that it's too soon to be squinting this far into the future. I'd be lying if I said I didn't understand. It's great being young and carefree. It's easy not having to think past tomorrow or that awesome pair of jeans you want to buy this weekend at the mall. Stalling, however, doesn't change the fact that life's runway is a lot shorter than you realize.

Set up a meeting with yourself. Put yourself through a Q-and-A session. Get a general feel for how you want your life to unfold. You don't have to have the name of your destination yet. You don't need to have all the routes planned. You don't even need to have specific dreams. Contrary to what you hear, not everyone does. Don't worry. Even if you're light on detail, stay strong on message. Get familiar with the process. Get those engines going.

As for those of you who want your face (and hands, don't forget your hands) to suggest you're forty when you're fifty, do the smart thing and get your plan in motion from now. Start taking care of that flawless young skin.

2

KNOWING THYSELF

("Sometimes it feels as if being myself
is the hardest thing to do.")

Why is it so important that we take a good look at ourselves?

Don't we frown on the me-me-me culture? Isn't it more altruistic to focus beyond self? And don't we already know enough about ourselves by the time we hit adulthood? After all, we've known ourselves longer than anyone. We know ourselves inside and out. Or do we?

Not a Drill. Not a Rehearsal.

Imagine that you're standing before a giant department store. It's huge—a hundred times the size of the biggest one you know. It's so vast you can't even see where it ends. From the moment you set foot through its doors, countless aisles beckon you with floor-to-ceiling shelves and racks, each filled with choices from the simple to the mind-blowing.

Then imagine finding out that the store is open for you and only you. No one else gets to come in while you're shopping. You can choose anything you want. Exciting, right? Then you're told that there are three hitches:

- You have a limited amount of time in which to shop.

- The return policy is replete with restrictions—some things will be harder to return than others. In some cases you may well be stuck with your choice.

- You only get one chance to do this.

What's your strategy? Do you shrug your shoulders, pick a random aisle and start strolling, hoping for something nice to jump out at you? Or do you pause to picture what it is you really want and then head toward the correct aisle (or department), wasting no time on the other tempting trinkets vying for your attention?

If you're still in your early twenties, this is you. How will you choose? How will you show up on your life's stage? How will you show up in this world?

As I suggested in chapter 1, glancing up at the road ahead is not only important, it's a sign of maturity. Whether you're ready or not, at some point you must consider your future. You must decide which signposts you need to follow. And while you should absolutely seek the help of others, ultimately you'll be making the journey alone.

But how do you know what you want, especially if you're fairly young? Aren't you just getting your first taste of life? How can you know that your choices are right for you? While there are no guarantees you'll hit bull's-eye, there is a way to ensure you get close enough: know who you are.

Crash Your Own Party

A friend of mine once shared a story about overhearing two ladies—strangers to each other—as they chatted politely while standing in line at a book fair in her city.

As they made small talk while waiting to file into the next author presentation, the older of the two shared her excitement about finally feeling free to embrace her true interests. "For years I strained myself to be open to what I thought were the 'right' things to like," she said to her new acquaintance. "I was even open to jazz. For twenty years!" she said with a howl. "That is so not me. But this," she said, waving her arms at the busy open-air convention filled with tented book-stalls, "this is me."

While this lighthearted anecdote is good for a chuckle, it drives home the point that you should never waste your time living some-one else's life. That's why the real secret to a happy life ultimately rests on how well you know—and honor—your true self. And there is nothing selfish about that. Being honest with yourself means being honest with those in your life. And that's the right thing to do.

Remember: the ability to achieve self-awareness is a leadership skill.

If you have an awareness of who you are at the core early in life, you almost can't help but make certain choices that naturally align with this foundation. In fact, it would make the New Year's Day goal-planning exercise a lot easier.

Before you make those important decisions, before you go shopping in that giant department store that is your life, sit with yourself a little and decide who you are. Once you know what feels good in your skin, your inner compass will automatically guide you to your true north. Going against it—sensing that shaking of the needle when you're off course—will instantly give you that *yuck* sensation that says something's not right.

But how does this personal insight manifest itself in everyday life?

On a practical level, knowing what's core for you will serve as your wrong-way sign when you're considering a route that's not good for you. I'm referring to the bigger decisions we make, like taking a job (even a fantastic one) simply because it pays more than your current one, even though it's not a good fit. Or settling down with a chain-smoking, chips-and-soda type of person when you know you want a mate who loves green smoothies and weekend hikes as much as you do. Or leaving the suburbs for the city when you cringe at the sound of sirens and chafe at the thought of not being able to pull into your own driveway.

But there is also a spiritual element to self-awareness. It's about knowing what makes your heart sink and what makes it soar, and being at peace with it. Keeping your true nature submerged is miserable work. Have you ever tried holding a ball under water? How long did it take before your muscles began to ache? Now imagine doing that your entire life.

Here's the thing. Introspection is the path to self-awareness. It sounds simple enough, but don't be fooled. This solitary exercise requires honesty. And honesty requires courage.

What's Your ZIP Code?

But there is good news.

While any self-audit is tough, it is meant to be a no-judgment zone. As you ask yourself questions, relax in the knowledge that there is no right or wrong answer. And if this proves to be particularly difficult for you, take the perspective of an observer and think of yourself in the third person. Once you're more relaxed and the process begins to flow more naturally, shift back to the first person. What's important is that you become conscious of yourself, learn how you're uniquely wired, and discover how you appear to others.

This is your acknowledgment of how life has shaped and molded you. Know how you "land on" or impact others in how you present yourself and what you say. Do others gravitate toward you? Or do they recoil? And do you have the emotional intelligence to ascertain why? What gets you revved up? What role or profession would feel like living in a second skin to you?

The answers are as personal and unique as your fingerprint.

For example, I know myself well enough to say that I am more of an order giver than an order taker. It's not that I can't execute. I wouldn't be where I am today were I incapable of seeing directives though to the end. However, I know that I am using my superpower when looking at the overall picture and using critical thinking to paint another.

This is where *my* genius lives.

This is my ZIP code. So why wouldn't I want to go home to it every day?

Reality Chat

Let's talk real life for a minute. No question about it, tough circumstances may influence your decision to take a job you're not exactly swooning over: a crushing student loan, a flat economy, family obligations. These and others are usually the culprits behind our choice of ill-fitting jobs or careers. They are the reasons we sometimes put our dream job in the luxury category. After all, we still gotta eat.

I get it. I, too, had similar concerns.

When I went hunting for that first job out of college, my school loan was my focus. Determined to get that monkey off my back, I took the first offer that came along, a job I admit was a relatively safe one. It was safe because it paid the bills and matched my skill set for the most part.

Don't get me wrong. I liked it enough. I didn't, however, consider aiming for something I was more passionate about. In my mind, that was a luxury I couldn't afford. But even today, in my heart I still wish I had taken that chance on myself. I was young. I was smart. Educated. And brimming with energy. I can only imagine where I'd be now had I let myself burst out from the starting blocks with that youthful vigor. I wish I had had more faith in myself back then. But I know that it's easy for me to say this today, now that my school loan is no longer the last thing I think of before going to sleep.

If this is you, I want to applaud you for making that incredibly adult decision of meeting your obligations and standing on your own two feet. Working to put yourself through college is a mark of determination; a badge of honor you should wear with pride. The experience will help you build muscles you never knew you had. It may even give you the mental edge over your competitors who did not have these pressures on their plate.

But I also want to plant a reminder in your head. While you go through this temporary phase of sacrifice—this personal tour of duty, if you will—you must keep an eye out for the right exit ramp. Ultimately, when your debts are under control and you have more wiggle room, you want to get back to your blueprint. You want a life you're dying to jump at each morning your alarm goes off.

As you go through these sample questions, ask yourself which option makes the corners of your mouth curl upward more:

- The unknown (e.g., living out of suitcase) or the predictable (e.g., eating cereal out of your favorite bowl each morning)?

- Working on a project-to-project basis or settling into the steadier routine of a more permanent role?

- Leading a team, understudying the leader, contributing as a team member, or working for yourself?

- Juggling several balls in the air or focusing on one or two at a time?

- Taking risks (be they financial, professional, or personal) or playing it safe?

- Carrying out directives or formulating them?

- Brainstorming out loud in a group or quietly on your own?

- Networking at a large event or cozy luncheon?

- Working toward smaller but immediate rewards or delaying gratification for possibly bigger outcomes?

- Sitting behind a desk or staying in motion?

- Finding a partner with your background (culture, education, ethnicity) or opening yourself to anyone as long as they can handle your freakishly long second toe?

- A constant carnival of friends and acquaintances or one or two besties?

- Suits or sweats?

- City or suburbs?

- Pet dog or goldfish?

By asking yourself these seemingly simple questions, you're actually piecing together bits and pieces of a unique mosaic, seen clearly in all its beauty once you step back and admire it from a distance.

Self-Awareness Tools

For some folks, self-awareness is something they happen upon later in life; they suddenly get it or see themselves or a situation for what it really is. But why wait? There are a couple of tools available to help you find it now.

Feedback

Seek feedback from people you admire and respect. Ask them how they view you in general. Then be more specific and ask them how they view your handling of certain situations. Let them know you want the truth. You may not like everything you hear, but you can only benefit from their perspective. And if it helps, remind yourself that no one is perfect.

Why is it so important to seek the opinion of others? Countless corporate cultures are negative feedback environments. In those settings, if you are doing what's expected of you, chances are you won't hear anything. That's because feedback tends to come in one variety: negative. As a result, individuals are often blindsided by the once-yearly review that focuses on how we got it all wrong. Worse yet are cultures where feedback is all but absent. Suddenly, you're being put on probation for something no one bothered to tell you had been an issue all along.

Consider constructive feedback from someone you trust as an annual checkup for your career or personal life. It's the way we improve as human beings when we're too busy or involved to see the warning signs of a problem arising.

In my own consultancy work, I often have to provide feedback on a client's blind spots. For example, I recently had to tell a CEO, "Heather," that her formidable personal assistant, while undeniably loyal and exceedingly competent as her gatekeeper, was no longer the best person for that position. She was, in fact, inadvertently blocking Heather's view of certain golden opportunities on the horizon.

This can happen when a company has either grown exponentially or changed direction, while the candidate originally hired for the position has remained stagnant. But because this individual had had Heather's back since the company's inception, Heather was blind to her assistant's limitations. The truth is, they both were.

It was not easy to share this insight with my client. Feedback can be upsetting at times. If done in the spirit of progress, however, it can also be rewarding. (PS. Heather's assistant was moved to a new position where she now thrives.) And as Hillary Rodham Clinton once reminded us, we should all "take criticism seriously but not personally." Too often, however, this is not the case, especially for women.

Journaling

So often we live on autopilot. We lose the connection to why we do what we do. Journaling is the discipline of putting your thoughts and feelings under the proverbial microscope. It helps us to focus less on what we're doing and more on how we're being.

To get into a real rhythm of journaling, decide that you're going to journal every day for a month. It sounds like a Herculean effort, but once you get started, journaling becomes something you look forward to. Knowing that you will spend at least a few minutes a day making observations or recording your random thoughts makes it easier to transition to meaningful self-discovery. But you must commit to doing this fairly regularly. Otherwise the results will be diluted.

Achieving fulfillment in our work means finding that sweet spot between where you flourish as a human being and the role you play every day. That match will not always be perfect, but it's an important alignment to aim for. The key is to know what it is you're reaching for. And the only way to get there is to get in touch with your core by asking certain questions.

Without getting too Zen, I want to share my own story about my first encounter with journaling as a young graduate student. I am an extrovert. Like others of my kind, I thrive on the energy of people interactions, engagement, and the 24-7 nature of the world we live in. This means that when I was younger, the thought of sitting alone for an extended period to quietly contemplate my navel ranked next to being trapped in an elevator during a power blackout just before lunch.

So when I found myself faced with an assignment to write a six-page personal history for a graduate class, I just knew that the universe was having a good chuckle at my expense.

To work on this assignment, I carved out some alone time—and not just an hour. *Days.* If you're a type A personality, you know that there's not enough double-sided tape in the world to make you sit still for that long. You feel you're doing nothing if you're merely being contemplative. It's time to rid yourself of that perception. This quiet time is an enormous investment in yourself and your future. It's an exercise that the truly successful engage in.

Ask yourself:

- Are you generally self-motivated?

- Would you say you're fairly disciplined?

- Do you see the value in daily rituals?

- How are you smart?

- How do you learn best?

- Are you impulsive? Or are you a planner?

- How do you handle change, especially the sudden kind?

- How do you react to pressure such as deadlines or conflict?

- Are you recognizable when you're angry or upset?

- Do you take criticism well?

- What have your defining moments been to date, and why do you consider them to be defining?

- Did those defining moments change your trajectory?

- What personal values came through?

- What patterns do you notice?

- Where are you now?

- Where do you want to be?

- What do you see as your obstacles?

Taking the time to get in touch with who you are, what you want, and why you want these things goes a long way to giving you clarity about your strengths, passions, goals, relationships, and purpose in life. While I initially bit my nails to the quick over this assignment, I found it to be one of the most rewarding exercises of my life. I laughed and cried in a wholly cathartic way. In the end, I produced twelve pages of personal history instead of the required six, and I found my raison d'être. Not only did I discover my "why," I discovered the joy and power of journaling and making lists.

Time is a horrible commodity to waste. Don't wait twenty years to figure out that the path you're on is not actually yours. The realization that you've been chasing someone else's dream can hit you with the subtlety of an ice-cold shower.

Take off your blinders, put down your phone, and get into some serious navel-gazing. You may be surprised at the real you waiting to be discovered.

3

GETTING OFF TO A GOOD START

("I can't believe I'm actually here!
Quick! What do I do?")

Nothing pumps adrenaline in your veins quite like acing those first few strides in your new journey.

Those important first steps include simple acts such as greeting your day. Each morning, I prime the twenty-four hours ahead of me by sitting quietly for a few minutes with a cup of hot coffee cradled in my hands and engaging in what, for me, is the secret sauce for life: expressing gratitude to God for all that I have. For as long as I can remember, I have begun each day thanking Him for the gift of life, for the joy of family, for the fellowship of friends, for the comfort of health, and for another chance to use the talents He gave me to help others.

But setting the tone for my day is about so much more than laying a foundation of gratitude. It's also about embracing habits that support clear thinking, efficiency, and a sense of control. To achieve this, I do the following:

- *Compose a to-do list last thing in the evening.* By now you know that I live by my lists. Without them I have no sense of bearing. I am a car without a steering wheel. But when I put my to-do list together, I relax in the knowledge that I already know how the following day will unfold, barring any unforeseen mishaps.

- *Consult said to-do list in the morning.* Once I stir from my slumber, I am ready to face the world. From appointments to deadlines to grocery shopping to making dinner (or not), it's all on my roadmap for the day. I am confident that I will hit the must-see marks because I've planned it all ahead of time. Now I'm following directions. If you're not in the habit of making lists, try it. Nothing gives you a confidence boost quite like that rush of crossing off an item that's been completed. Sometimes, if I've finished a task not originally on the list, I'll write it down anyway just for the thrill of crossing it out. Within seconds of doing this, I feel like a winner.

- *Ensure that my space is clutter-free.* By "space," I mean my desk, my car, and even my handbag. (And if you can get your home clutter-free, too, you're way ahead of the game.) Precious time wasted searching for notes, keys, bills—anything—is time we could have spent getting that assignment done, paying our bills on time, exercising, or spending time with family and friends. Make order and structure part of your everyday life. Don't tolerate piles of random paper and envelopes. Don't tolerate piles of anything for that matter. Give each item a home. Get a filing cabinet, then make files for your paperwork (bills, etc.). Sort out that closet. Ensure that everything in there flatters ·you. Get rid of excess. No longer wear or use it? Give it away or donate it to a good cause. Once you've experienced the lightness of a space that's clean and free of distractions, you'll understand what virtue there is in being organized.

When order and purpose are the starting blocks to any task, a sense of clarity will fuel you to the finish line. This working formula is transferable to the bigger picture of your life. It means that even when all the stars are not aligned, you still have the power to refocus and reset the tone because you have established a foundation of order to support you.

Choosing Your Mind-Set

Many might say that my first mentor—my mother—did not exactly have the right start. Born in the 1930s in the segregated South, Anne

Nero could have easily chosen to face life with a negative outlook. And no one would have blamed her for it.

But she did not allow the weeds of bitterness from her childhood experiences in the Jim Crow era to take root in her heart and choke her natural curiosity and creativity. Instead, she changed the game and took as much control over her life as she could. She practiced yoga before it became fashionable. She walked and stretched for health. She even got her college degree.

I didn't appreciate until I was much older the powerful mind-set she must have adopted in order to do all this. Today, I marvel at what she overcame, not just as an African American but also as an African American woman, and as a woman, period.

Young Anne gave herself the best start possible by adopting a positive attitude. She graced all whom she met and experiences she encountered with a gracious acceptance and openness that belied her foundation of limitations. I would often walk through our front door to see one of my friends chatting with her in our living room. They hadn't come for me. They were there to see her. How did she do this? How did she win the admiration of so many? Simple. She understood the art of nailing that all-important first impression.

New Job? Congratulations!

Getting off to a good start in your career or new job is critical. While it's not impossible to change someone's initial perception of you, it's also not easy. Human nature is such that we tend to cling to the first impression we have about people. Once it's there—and especially if we share it with others—we go looking for things that validate our initial assessment for the sake of being right. This makes giving a poor first impression an obstacle that we should, and can, avoid in the first place.

It would be easy to set down a laundry list of dos and don'ts here and call it a day. But creating a positive impression involves so much more. It requires a great deal of self-awareness to handle nuanced behavior. It demands thought and care and encompasses the ability to act as an observer—to see ourselves as others see us. It means being able to stand in someone else's shoes and hear our own words as they land in that person's ears.

Prepare

Being prepared is critical on two fronts:

1. **It Helps You to Relax**

   First, the better prepared you are, the more in control of your first-day jitters you'll be (in theory). Take it from someone who has made a lifelong habit of preparing for almost everything she does. Once you know you've done all the behind-the-scenes work you can (hours of rehearsing, making notes, doing extra research), relax and have fun.

   My approach is the same no matter the task at hand. Before I make a presentation or give a public speech, for instance, I spend hours studying my notes and rehearsing its delivery. Right before the event— even the night before, if possible—I scout out the venue. I literally walk onto the stage before the empty auditorium. I pay attention to the feel of the floor beneath my heels. I rest my hand on the podium. I get comfortable with the lighting. I stand there and take in the size of the room, the smell of it, and visualize the seats filled with people looking at me. And I picture myself delivering a speech worthy of a standing ovation before an enthusiastic audience.

   Now and then, however, even this level of preparation is not enough. In the hour before showtime my heart can still go racing. If I'm prepared, I tell myself that I'm nervous because I'm taking the opportunity seriously. But if I'm still anxious after all the aforementioned tricks and fixes, I'll remedy it by rechanneling my energy. I'll go to the restroom, where it's quiet, or stand backstage and tell myself that I'm excited about what I'm about to share with the audience and that I know the material inside out. I tell myself that I'm about to have the most exhilarating experience.

And if *that* doesn't work, I'll hold a cup of hot water in my hands to calm myself or stand in what is known as the "power pose" with my hands on my hips. And for my final trick, I'll reach into my handbag for the little bottle of lavender oil I carry with me and rub it on my wrists or through my fingers. These are the tools and techniques that I reach for.

What does your preparation strategy look like?

2. It Shows Your Good Intentions

The second reason to prepare is to show your new colleagues, supervisors, and managers that you have done your homework and are serious about your new job. This doesn't mean that you never crack a smile, of course. You can be fun and lighthearted as long as you're always serious about your work. You want to send the message that you're someone they can count on because no one is going to outwork you. How and what should you prepare? Doing your due diligence means finding out anything and everything you can:

- With whom will you be working?

- What do the bios of your company and division leaders reveal?

- What did you find out on LinkedIn about the people who used to work there? For example, how long did they stay? Do you see a pattern?

- What are the company's headlines in terms of successes and obstacles, both internally and industry-wide?

- How are decisions made? Who tends to make them?

- How does the company make a profit? It's not enough to limit your knowledge to your functional area. Have at least a basic understanding of how your company makes its payroll.

- What does its latest earnings look like?

- What initiatives is the company involved in?

- What are the names of its largest customers?

- What do you know about its new product launches and charitable event sponsorships?

Knowledge of any information in the public domain is useful. That way, not only will you be able to participate in a more informed way on day one, but what you hear and observe will make more sense to you. More importantly, you will make more sense to them.

I once delivered a presentation that fell flat because I let it. I had not drilled down enough on content. I didn't find out as much about my audience as I should have. I was more focused on me, thinking about what *I* wanted to tell *them* rather than what they needed to hear. I didn't ask myself what they would find valuable or what their current concerns were. In the end, I didn't prepare information they wanted in exchange for giving me their valuable time. It's not that what I delivered was awful. It was simply misplaced. What would have had another audience on their feet applauding had this one checking the time and yawning.

Look, Watch, Listen

Imagine it's your first week at the new job. Maybe it's your first job out of college or graduate school. Perhaps it's five years later and you've accepted a great offer at a new firm. You made it through five rounds of interviews and completely nailed it. What can you do to ensure a good start?

Become the observer.

I'm not suggesting you refrain from speaking or trusting your own instincts about your knowledge base. But think about it. We learn much more by listening than we do by talking. At this early juncture with the company, it's important that you step back to assess this new environment. Take the time to observe your surroundings.

- Is it casual and open? Are subordinates free to address the boss by his or her first name?

- Is it more buttoned up? Mr., Ms., or Mrs. plus last name only, please?

- Is the culture somewhat passive-aggressive? Do people nod their heads in agreement in a meeting for good optics, only to then become unreachable afterward when it's time to follow through?

Strong powers of observation will enable you to read the culture and fit in. This is particularly important when working overseas where the culture may differ greatly from what you're used to. Understand that in no way would I encourage anyone to be inauthentic in the workplace. But, as the newcomer on a team of colleagues, you have to acknowledge the framework you're stepping into in order to adapt to it and maximize your contribution.

How's That Outfit Working for You?

Do most women at your company wear suits? High heels? Are the heels walking-on-the-balls-of-your-feet high or more conservative?

Is the dress overall business casual? How casual is casual? Do those at the professional level dress differently from the women in support roles? Are there dress-down Fridays? Should you ever wear jeans?

If you have a female boss, take cues from her. If she does not wear pants to the office, it doesn't mean you can't, but it does mean you should wear appropriately formal pants or slacks. Based on what you've observed, how should you dress?

Obviously, there is an enormous spectrum of dress codes that dictate what's acceptable where. At some small start-ups, for example, you might be completely out of sync if you show up in business attire. Gauge the vibe and ensure that you are in line with expectations.

Looking Around

Like your family, every organization has its own dynamics when it comes to power. Unfortunately, this is not the sort of information you'll find in a company manual. And unless a coworker volunteers this information, only time and keen observation will reveal all. It would be wise to study the landscape. That doesn't mean you should go around asking for information about people around you, but it does mean you should listen for clues as to who the decision-makers are in your organization and who has the most influence. This will become helpful to you as you gain more responsibility.

Don't Forget Your Manners

While this kind of basic advice may sound obvious—or even silly— it's important in getting off to a good start.

Extending Courtesy

It may sound as old-fashioned as licking stamps, but *please* and *thank you* still go a long way, as do thank-you notes and emails like this:

Dear Sharon,

Thank you for taking the extra time to explain the ABC Account and the new sales pitch that you're working on. I look forward to hearing more about it when we meet again next Tuesday.

Sincerely,
Lisa Brooks-Greaux

Using a smile, firm handshake, solid eye contact, and the person's name when greeting them or ending a meeting are also good signs of engagement.

Showing Respect

You should be demonstrating utter respect for all your new colleagues. If you're joining as a leader or manager, it's equally important to show the same regard for your new subordinates. Assume that their expertise and the place they have carved out in this organization are worthy of your admiration. Because of the journey they have endured, chances are your superiors hold them in high esteem. You can hope to win their respect upon your arrival, but in more cases than not, when you show them this consideration first, it quickly becomes mutual.

Oozing Humility

Now is not the time to be patting yourself on the back. How many times have you been in a meeting with a know-it-all who soon becomes the class bore? They lose impact on their audience because they don't choose their moments wisely. They fade into the background and become white noise.

When you're the new kid on the block—no matter what position you've been hired into—humility about what you know and don't know will earn you much greater cooperation from those around you. Even those who can boast a 3.9 GPA from an Ivy League university would do well to refrain from broadcasting it. Rather, show your colleagues that you've got the right stuff with your brilliant performance and ability to deliver results.

Making Connections

If you're feeling shy or concerned about how to break the ice with strangers, remember that folks love to talk about themselves. *Everyone* likes to feel important. Ask questions casually, without being nosy. Ask about their jobs, what they are currently working on, how long they've been in the industry, or what they studied at school. Do they have children? Listen to their answers and take it from there. There are many ways to get the conversation started, and the best way to make a great start is to make connections.

Communicating Like a Boss

How you communicate says a lot about you. But what about communicating with your new boss? Do you know how she prefers to receive information?

Week one is the perfect time to speak with her about what works best. Being detail-oriented is one of the traits women are known for. So double down on it. Ask your boss:

- How often would you like to receive updates—weekly, twice weekly, or daily?

- Are you a phone person or would you rather have face-to-face meetings?

- If it's written updates you want, would you prefer bullet-point briefs or detailed memos?

- Is email the only option or are you fine with texts, too?

Doing this immediately is one way of showing your boss that you have what it takes to be a consummate professional, and it sets the tone for how you like to do business. Remember, too, that it behooves you to help make your boss's job easier and make him or her look better. After all, this is the person who's going to have some influence over your destiny on the job.

But what about other stakeholders? Who else will be impacted by your work? Who will your allies be? What about your peers? What would they say about you if asked? Your boss is not the only person who needs to be saying good things about you.

Words Are Tools. Wield Them Wisely.

Use your head when it comes to communication in general, regardless of whom you're interacting with. Most work-related communication takes place via email. This can be tricky, though, because tone and nuance can easily be lost. This can lead to misunderstandings, misrepresentation, misinformation, hurt feelings, and an unnecessary mess. If this can happen with even our friends, imagine then the repercussions in the workplace.

Think Before You Send

Emails get forwarded—a lot. Once you hit send, you have no control over who will read your message.

Read and reread your message before you release it. As much as you can, ensure that nothing you've written can be misconstrued as demeaning to anyone. How's your tone? Is it aligned with your intention? Read it from the point of view of the recipient. Have you taken the office politics and dynamics into consideration? How could your message be misinterpreted? One word of caution: As the new employee, and even as a seasoned leader, you *never* want to throw anyone under the bus, even if you're in the right. While you don't want to be paranoid when communicating within your company, you want to be careful.

Let's Be Clear

Take your time when crafting your message. Recheck your words to ensure that you have conveyed the information you want to. Get rid of any ambiguity. Clarity is key when speaking and writing. Ask yourself these questions:

- Have you clearly stated the intent of the email?

- What about your call for action? Do recipients know exactly what you want them to do (e.g., provide feedback, give approval, make an introduction, schedule a follow-up meeting)?

- Do you indicate deadlines (if any) clearly?

- Does the email seem dense? Unappealing to the eye? Or have you made good use of bullet points, numbering, spacing, and white space?

Using the active voice over the ambiguous passive voice not only makes you appear more confident and competent, but it leads to well-crafted emails that will help make a strong first impression and get noticed. Take your time to draft and redraft. The effort will pay off. Master the art of clarity and you'll be the one they remember.

Check, Please

Proofread, proofread, and proofread again. Nothing says "I don't care" or "You're not important enough for me to care" like an email riddled with typos and sloppy grammatical errors. While mistakes happen, certain kinds are inexcusable. If you can, put your draft aside for a few minutes or longer and go back to it with fresh eyes. And whatever you do, be particularly vigilant when it comes to people's names. Jane could actually be Jayne, just as Brian could be Bryan. Remember: nothing is more precious to an individual than hearing or seeing their name.

Get it right. Even if it's a fairly common name, you will never be in the wrong for asking how it's spelled.

Following Through

One thing that will set you apart from the rest is your ability to follow up on communication and tasks, whether you're the recipient or originator of an email or letter.

Never assume that email *sent* means email *read*.

Let me repeat that: never assume that email *sent* means email *read*.

With the average person receiving dozens of emails a day—even hundreds in some cases—expect that your recipient has other correspondence to attend to. Make a habit of asking them to confirm that they've received yours.

Likewise, always extend the same courtesy. Even a simple "thank-you" will do. This ties up loose ends and keeps you both honest. In other words, no one can convincingly make the claim that they didn't receive your directive/request/update, nor can they say that you didn't acknowledge theirs. And if you haven't received a reply within a reasonable amount of time, follow up with a friendly phone call, text, or email.

Nothing is worse than having your boss ask you for an update on, for example, the estimate promised by Vendor X, only to be forced to tell him or her that you don't know. You don't know, you go on to explain, because the vendor never got back to you on your request for said estimate.

While you can feel somewhat secure knowing that you did as your boss asked, the reality is your boss won't care that it was the vendor who technically dropped the ball first. All they will see is that you didn't pick it up.

Developing a Reputation

Part of creating a good first impression lies in demonstrating your willingness to jump in, roll up your sleeves, and get it done, whatever "it" is. In other words, become known for being a true team player.

Roll with It

That means being flexible, open-minded, and amenable to any and all assignments—even those you might perceive to be more appropriate for subordinates. Think about it from your employer's point of view. Maybe having you pore over arcane databases and create massive spreadsheets will give you great foundational experience for a role in forecasting future industry trends in your next assignment.

In fact, it's possible that your boss may be intentional in helping you gain exposure to various facets of the organization in order to give you broader responsibilities down the road. Or he or she may be running you through an audition, secretly testing you to see how much of a team player you really are. Who knows?

Ask for More

Do you find that you're not being fully utilized? Do you know deep down that you could take on more work? Then don't just sit there—raise your hand. Volunteer to take ownership of an action that comes up in a meeting. Or approach your overwhelmed boss or colleague and tell them you have additional bandwidth. Offer to shoulder some of their load if that would be appropriate. Who doesn't appreciate an offer of help? Not only does it prove that you're industrious, but it shows that you're paying attention.

The flip side of that coin is to be approachable—again, open-minded—so that a boss or colleague will feel like they can, and should, ask you to play a role in meeting a deadline, preparing a presentation, or brainstorming a strategy. If you give off the vibe that you are unwilling or uninterested in participating, you will ultimately get boxed out.

Prevailing with Common Sense

If you've come this far—through university, graduate school, or years in the working world—it should be safe to assume that you have some common sense. There are several best practices that fall into the common-sense category:

Assume Nothing

Everything is not as it seems. This is particularly important to remember when it comes to the new company's culture. It's better to find out the facts rather than to proceed on an assumption. Making assumptions—especially when you are new to an organization and more likely to misinterpret—can be an especially hazardous mistake.

Be Honest

It's always better to come clean that you don't know how to do something than to silently take it on and then struggle to deliver—or not deliver at all. You may end up embarrassing yourself, frustrating your team, or, worse, causing unnecessary cost to the company. Set your ego aside. Admitting to your shortcomings is not a sign of weakness but a show of consideration for the company and confidence in your ability and willingness to learn. If you've been assigned a task for which you feel unprepared even after exhausting all your resources (YouTube, Google, and go-to friends), circle back to your boss and ask for more clarification. Let him know you want to do a good job.

Be Conscientious

Put—your—phone—away. Texting while working is a lot like texting and driving: both can land you in deep trouble. We all have commitments and obligations outside of our work lives, and if we put in fifty hours or more a week at the office, we undoubtedly have to make or take personal calls there. But if your boss or colleagues are aware of them, then they may be too frequent. And unless engaging in social media is part of your job, save those personal tasks for outside work hours.

Be Extremely Conscientious

Make a good impression on your superiors.

Is your boss already at the office when you arrive at 8:30 a.m.? Then try getting in at 8:00. She's there at 8:00 a.m.? Make sure you're there by 7:30. Is your boss still at his desk when you leave at 5:30 p.m.? Hold back until 6:00. He's still there at 6:30? Try for 7:00 p.m.

This is not hard-and-fast, of course, as the scope of your responsibility, number of projects you are involved in, and a myriad of other factors come into play. The point is that you want to be seen as making the effort. And while you don't want to sit there and pretend to be working, nothing gets under a boss's (or colleague's) skin more than seeing someone float in late and dash out early when the rest of the team is breaking its collective back. That's a sure way to get booted off the island.

I once met a girl from Toronto who, on learning one Sunday night in January that a blizzard was due to hit the city the following morning, got in to work two hours early just so she could avoid being even fifteen minutes late. She was the first one there, at 6:00 a.m. Twenty minutes later, the executive vice president walked in. When it was time for her to leave years later, he gave her a golden letter of recommendation.

But even in today's corporate world, where flexible hours are now the norm, be careful about not abusing the company's generosity. Human nature remains largely unchanged when it comes to optics. Always give more than is expected of you. It doesn't matter if everyone leaves promptly at 5:00 p.m. or always extends their lunch break by a few extra minutes. Do right by your company and stand out from the crowd. You'll be duly rewarded for your conscientiousness.

Protecting Your Brand

Think of yourself as a brand. Make sure that your public image does not suggest that you lead a double life. Don't recklessly share pictures or information on social media about yourself that you wouldn't want your mother or baby sister to know. If it's going to hurt their eyes, it'll crush your career when your bosses see it. And see it they will. Checking a candidate's or employee's profile has become standard practice. So don't overshare. Don't talk about how you woke up on Sunday morning in a stranger's apartment after a night of binge drinking. Just don't do it. Good judgment is imperative in an era in which information cannot be erased. Learn the practice of prudence. It is a virtue good leaders possess.

Acting with Intention

Acting with intention entails thinking before you make a move, interacting with kindness, and treating all colleagues with respect—not just those who can further your career. This is yet another quality of character that leaders look for in their younger associates.

Getting along with other people—of all sorts—is ultimately the key to success in this world. Starting off at a new job is no different. For many of us, it's easy to build rapport with people like ourselves—people who share our sport team affiliations, love of gardening, and (you fill in the blank). But since we don't choose our coworkers or bosses, how do we go about building rapport with people with whom we have absolutely nothing in common? How are you, a twenty-something bookworm supposed to talk to that much older sports fan on your team?

Fortunately, building rapport is a learnable skill. If you don't know how to do it, shadow someone who does. Watch how they work a room. Listen to their opening lines. Watch their body language. Or take a course and learn. Or watch YouTube videos on the topic. (Yes, there are videos on this!) Once you've learned this skill, you'll have the other key driver to success: the ability to influence people.

Asking for Directions

It's an old joke that while men won't ask for directions, we ladies do and think nothing of it. To us, it just makes sense. Well, here's some good news. Getting "directions" on the job is no different from getting them on the road. It makes sense in both scenarios. You don't want to waste time getting lost and retracing your steps. So go right ahead. Embrace the stereotype and use it to your advantage.

You're Being Paid to Know

Some may push back and suggest that asking a lot of questions reveals how much you *don't* know. They wonder if this could inadvertently create a bad first impression.

They're wrong.

Asking questions is a sign of humility and strength. It's the key to getting off on the right foot. If you take a deeper view and think of how your new boss or colleagues might interpret this, then you will understand how it works. Gathering information shows that you're engaged in the conversation. It shows that you are analyzing what you're hearing and that you're attempting to make connections. It shows an eagerness to "unpack your bags" and get settled in. And it shows a determination to become the company's newest asset.

Take it from someone who hires talent for a living. When I interview a candidate on behalf of my company or client, I rank attitude over intelligence almost every time. And while I do factor in the person's skill level and experience, I first want to know three things:

1. How trainable they are

2. How they approach obstacles

3. How well they play with others

Try These for Starters

But if you're secretly concerned about appearing unskilled, ignorant, or just plain dumb, don't worry. You're not alone. We all get that way sometimes. Until you get the hang of showing a little vulnerability at the workplace without feeling compromised, develop a vocabulary for asking questions.

For example, say you're in a meeting early on in your tenure at your firm. You have no idea what's going on in the room but know that you need to gain an understanding. And fast. Don't just sit there and hope to figure it out. Speak up and put it out there.

Here are some great openers:

- Do you have some examples of how that new system is supposed to work?

- Could you give me some more detail about those trends you just described?

- What does success for this project look like in your eyes?

If you are asked to perform a task that you aren't sure you know how to do, try this line of questioning:

- Would you give me some guidance here so I make sure I'm starting this in a format that works for you?

- Is there a template that you've used for this type of project in the past?

- How do you suggest I approach the (you fill in the blank)?

- Who else on the team might have some input on the project?

- Where can I go for background information on this project?

Think about it from your boss's perspective. These questions sound impressive coming from the new kid on the block. In fact, your boss may begin to worry if you don't have at least a short list of questions as you get settled in. Take advantage of the fact that your superiors know you will need some time to navigate the learning curve.

In the end, at work and in life, people are generally happy to help or share information with someone they perceive to be friendly and open to instruction and learning. Beginning a new job or career can be fraught with challenges, but it is also an exciting time. So put on a smile and can-do attitude, and show your new colleagues that you are deserving of their trust and respect.

Think smart. Act smart. Nail that first impression.

4

ASKING

("I'm an intelligent, strong woman.
Why is this so hard for me?")

It's a Saturday morning and I've already begun tackling my week-end chores.

I walk through my front door, my arms laden with bags of groceries as I struggle to make it to the kitchen in one trip. Before I can even drop my keys and purse on the first table I pass by, Carl calls out to me from the living room, where he's on a ladder fixing a light in the ceiling.

"Lisa! You're back already," he says. "Great. Would you give me a hand with something here?"

My first instinct is to react with a huff. I think the world of this man but am amazed that he could even think of asking me for help when it's obvious that I'm in the middle of a task of my own with no third hand to spare. But just as I'm about to fire off a retort, the researcher in me kicks in and I switch to observer mode. That's when I realize that I have just witnessed an example of one of the biggest differences between men and women in the workplace.

Men ask. Women don't.

This is not the kind of asking discussed in chapter 1, which involves seeking information for the sake of edification. This is about asking someone for something that benefits us, whether it be in the form of some kind of action, effort, or distribution of resources. It has been well documented that, by and large, men have less of an issue with this. In fact, asking for what they want comes quite naturally to most of them. Women, on the other hand, would rather drink shards of glass.

Why?

It has little to do with pride, if anything. Instead, it has much more to do with how we're socialized and, probably to a larger extent, our sense of self-worth. Women naturally hesitate to "inconvenience" others, preferring instead to play hero (in this case, heroine) or, worse, martyr. Instead of saying we need help—which is another way of saying no, we cannot accomplish task X under the given parameters—we choose to suffer behind the scenes. We constantly talk ourselves out of approaching someone with a request that could make our lives significantly easier, even if we are completely justified in making the request. And if we do muster the courage to speak up, we only begin to breathe once we've uttered the words and proved to ourselves that there is life after asking.

So . . . why not ask?

The Natural State of Asking

Expressing what we want or need is something we learn as children: "I want this," "I want that," or "Can I have that?" Sound familiar? More importantly, does it feel familiar? We learned this behavior at such an early age that it seems natural—almost a mantra. Even when we were told no, most of us were not dissuaded. As children, it didn't seem to faze us. Remember asking Mom for something and then asking Dad if she turned you down? (This, of course, was a punishable offense.)

Children aren't concerned by the first, second, or even third denial. They don't take the rejection personally. Instead, they look for alternative and creative ways to get what they want. They reframe the question or suggest alternatives. They tell you what's in it for you if you acquiesce. They persevere, sometimes relentlessly. Children aren't worried about being judged by others for asking for things. In fact, they are often brazen in their requests as they become single-minded in the pursuit of their end goal.

This goes for boys *and* girls.

What Changes?

What happens, then, as girls become young adults? When do young women lose their nerve to speak up and ask for what they want?

Why do they self-edit? When do they begin to feel too unworthy to state their case?

As they grow up, children learn that not all of their wants and needs can be met instantaneously. But in the workplace today there is a large and growing gap between the behavior of men and women when it comes to asking for things, whether it's funding or personnel or support from upper management.

Well, here's the headline to this story: *it's having a profoundly negative impact on women's careers.*

A Different Kind of Diet

Several reasons come to mind when thinking about the roots of this dichotomy. The main culprit? You guessed it: the way we are socialized as women.

For starters, young girls may receive subtle messages that they shouldn't ask for more servings of food because they might get fat or because they should leave some for other family members. "Let's not be greedy!" they're told. This is the essence of their conditioning—think of others first. As they grow up, girls are taught, subliminally, of course, that they can and should make do with what they have (and be grateful for it, to boot). The list is long but repetitive: Good girls graciously accept what they're given. Good girls are agreeable. They don't show displeasure. They don't challenge. And they most certainly do not engage in assertive behavior like (cue small gasp) asking.

Instead, good girls are expected to smile and put the needs of others first. This is the type of caring behavior that gets rewarded, heralded, and, sadly, communicated to our daughters and young women in general. This, I should add, includes not feeling free to say no to requests that are made of us. How many times have we agreed to accommodate others in the name of "a simple favor" when we don't have the time, energy, or desire to?

Far too often, if we're being honest.

Yet, nine times out of ten, within seconds of saying yes to the request, that heavy feeling of resentment begins to grow in our gut.

And while we'd like to think the other person is the genesis of our resentment, we know they're not.

We are.

"That's not very nice, young lady."
It's no secret that being "demanding" as a woman is portrayed as unattractive. In fact, it's viewed as the opposite of ladylike or conciliatory. We see this message reinforced in television, print ads, and other forms of media, as well as in popular culture. Think of the stereotype of the aggressive and demanding woman who is tough to work for or a nightmare to be in a relationship with. Let's face it—society doesn't exactly give us a lot of wiggle room.

Is it any wonder, then, that we hesitate to ask for what we want? Is it any surprise that we usually choke on saying the word *no*, even if it would mean giving our overloaded schedule some much-needed breathing space? All of these subtle—and not so subtle—messages can sabotage women and chip away at our confidence.

"I'll take care of it!"
As a result, I have seen many women become one-woman bands.

They make do with the meager resources provided to complete a project, not wanting to inconvenience anyone with requests for more talent, time, or treasure. Meanwhile, their male colleagues—who, by the way, remain oblivious to this great divide—go about their work completely unencumbered by these thoughts. They decisively request more at will and often receive exactly what they ask for. So again I wonder, why don't we ask?

Our Own Worst Enemy

What many of us have experienced is that self-editing voice. It's the internal tape that says, "You don't need that." Or the voice that worries about what other people will think. "Will I be perceived as arrogant or a diva by asking for more? Will people think I can't handle the project myself or that I'm in over my head? Or, worse yet, will they think I'm weak or unqualified for the position, period? If I ask for help, will my boss hand the job to someone else?" Sometimes we are paralyzed by the voice telling us that our request will be turned down. "I'll look like a fool," you tell yourself. And, far too often, we give that voice power without even verifying its accuracy.

"I'll be your superhero."

There's another reason we women don't ask for help or for what we need. I call it the *superhero syndrome*. Being self-reliant is an admirable quality, but we all need the self-awareness to recognize when it's time to reach out.

Everyone needs help at some point. *Everyone.*

Naturally, we want to be able to say we got the job done with as few resources as possible. We want it known that we were able to complete the project without additional funding or personnel and in record time. But at what cost?

While I applaud this type of work ethic in certain circumstances (and you should always do your best), I would argue that it is not a sustainable practice. Not only can it lead to burnout, but it sets a precedent for misallocating resources in the future. Worse, it can also set you up for unrealistic expectations where your future performance is concerned. It's a lie needlessly perpetuated.

More Than Just a Number

Women pay a severe price for this pattern of behavior. With each failure to assert themselves, their self-esteem is eroded bit by bit. Before long, resentment and bitterness take root.

In the seminal book *Women Don't Ask*, authors Linda Babcock and Sara Laschever outline several consequences of this defeatist habit.

Not surprisingly, chief among them is not asking for the salary or compensation we deserve. Exploring the causes and, more importantly, the implications of our failure to ask for what we need, this book has been a bestseller for more than a decade. No surprise why. The results of the extensive research presented are both compelling and sad. If you're the parent of young daughters, it would behoove you to read it. And if you're a young woman just starting out in life and know that not asking is your Achilles heel, I'd urge you to read this book and clear your hurdle now.

Raising the Question

Perhaps nothing gives women cold sweats and weeks of sleepless nights more than negotiating their salary, whether at the onset of being hired for a job or in the context of asking for a raise.

My own research shows that while a female candidate will, on hearing her proposed salary, thank the interviewer and ask for her starting date, the male candidate will usually thank the interviewer and then add the "but" part of the sentence. As in, "Thanks for the offer, *but* I really had X in mind."

Then it's off to the negotiating table they go.

Meanwhile, our agreeable female graduate, while thrilled to have a job, knows deep down that she has just acquiesced. Suddenly, she feels that proverbial pebble in her shoe. The loss is about more than money. Had she attempted to negotiate even a little, she would have gained the respect of the company for having shown her sense of self-worth. She would be sending the message that she's aware of what she has to offer and that other companies might be, too.

If this is you, do yourself a favor and break this crippling habit now.

At the time of writing this in late 2018, women are still earning only seventy-seven cents to every dollar men earn. But this is not surprising when you consider that only 7 percent of women even negotiate for their pay when offered a job. That is a staggering statistic that should give everyone pause. Think about the compounding impact of that first failure to ask over a thirty-five-year career—the extra 3 percent salary you may have gotten. Subsequent raises or new salaries go on to reflect the deficit of that starting salary and come up short each time.

Before you know it, you're near to retirement and wondering what went wrong.

Rewriting the Script

As a woman, I'm here to tell you that everything is negotiable. Let me repeat that: *everything is negotiable.*

Whether it's your job or some aspect of your personal life (yes, even a prenuptial agreement), you must ask for what you want, even if it makes you feel like you've been caught in a downpour and are now sitting in sopping wet clothes. No doubt about it, fighting for yourself can feel like miserable work with a major ick factor. But with a little research, regular practice, and lots of deep breathing, you can learn to feel comfortable at the negotiating table, especially if you know your requests are fair. And if you don't want to do it for your pocket, do it for your self-esteem.

The good news is that until you feel more at ease with discussing raw numbers, you can ask for other considerations.

Have a list ready. Here are some things you can ask for:

- More vacation time
- The ability to work from home
- Flexible hours for more family time
- Tuition reimbursement for advanced degrees
- Opportunities for professional development paid for by the company

Negotiate Early

The best time to negotiate is at the beginning, when someone wants you the most. If they refuse to negotiate even a little, they're showing you who they are and, more importantly, how they regard you. In that case, you're being given a blessing in disguise. Better to find out early on how much or how little you're valued.

As is usually the case for any conversation, it's more about how you say something than what you say. Don't wing it. Practice your pitch in front of the mirror or with a trusted friend or mentor. For example, you could say with sincerity and the appropriate body language: "That offer does sound good. Thank you! But my research shows that people in this field at my level of experience are getting XX. Would you take this into consideration?" If they say they'll have to get back to you, smile confidently and say: "Great! I really look forward to hearing from you. Thank you." If in your next meeting they confirm that they're not in a position to negotiate at the moment, then it's up to you to decide whether you want to move on or not. If, however, you still wish to accept, you might try saying: "I understand and really appreciate your honesty. Could we then agree to look at it six months from now?"

So important is this life skill of being an advocate for yourself that I present Babcock and Laschever's book to my MBA students on the first day of class. I urge them to read it cover to cover.

Then I set an assignment. I tell them that for one entire week, they are to ask strangers for something every day, at least once a day, be it an object (e.g., a pen) or act of service (e.g., help with carrying something). And I ask them to record how they felt after their request was accepted or denied (e.g., surprised, liberated, rejected).

Once the first week is over, I tell them to take it a notch up and keep going for the duration of the course. In my most recent class, one student—a male—went as far as to ask his boss for a raise. He shared with the class the story of a female colleague gasping at his bold move and saying that in her thirteen years with the company she had never asked for a raise. Not even once.

My female Muslim students in the same class had a particularly fun time with this assignment, finding it increasingly easy with each passing week to put their requests out there. "We should have learned this sooner!" one said, her eyes sparkling with a sense of genuine surprise.

Another student in the same class approached me after the term ended to ask me what she could have done to get an A instead of the A- I had given her. While I admired her ambition for excellence, I had no choice but to be a good teacher and honor her with honesty.

"Easy," I said with a smile. "You could have jumped on this sooner and asked me this question during the term when you could have done something about it." While my student didn't get her solid A, in my mind she got an even better reward: a lesson that will serve her well in what I know will be a successful life.

As for our brave student who asked his boss for better compensation, you may be wondering whether or not he got his raise. He did.

Why Practice Asking?

First, it makes us women aware of the fact that we are not natural askers. Second, by practicing the art of asking, we become comfortable with feeling uncomfortable. Because the reality is simple: if you don't ask, the answer will always be no. And that could mean missing out on important opportunities that could shape your life. Can you really afford the potential opportunity cost of remaining silent?

But ask and you might just hear *yes*.

Even if you're turned down, what's the worst that can happen? Disappointment? That's just life. Hurt pride? That's just ego talking. At least you won't have to live with the nagging "what if" of not knowing what could have happened in X or Y situation had you just opened your mouth and engaged your vocal cords.

Take a moment for a quick exercise right now.

Think back to all those times you sat on those burning requests. Make a list of them. Don't leave anything out. How did you talk yourself out of asking for help? Or for more resources? Or for something you wanted that wasn't even on the table to begin with? Did you even give asking a second thought? Don't you wish now that you had been brave enough to try, even if the answer had been no? And do you really want this list to grow any longer?

Mea Culpa

I am not lecturing from the pulpit but speaking as one who has sat among you learning this truth the hard way, many, *many* times over. I'll share one experience here.

Twelve years ago, when I was working at a Fortune 500 company, my boss gave me a significant assignment to spearhead. The project—creating a training program for network engineers—was a highly visible one. Because engineering was not my field, I had a sea of eyes on me. This was your classic stretch assignment. For that alone I was excited to take the lead.

But in my enthusiasm and appreciation for the opportunity to show my talent, I neglected to ask for the necessary financial resources and additional personnel crucial to the project's success. I was intent on proving that I could be that superhero who would bring the project in under budget and on time. I wanted to be the person who could do what others couldn't.

In my quest to prove my superhero status, I overwhelmed my team with impossible deadlines and budget constraints. Behind the scenes, my stress level overflowed into my personal life. I subjected my poor husband, family, and friends to weeks of unnecessary whining and venting. I became the person you want to dodge at all costs. In the end, my team and I completed the project on time and with the resources given. The company was ecstatic.

But I could barely manage a mental high five.

Bland Victory

I was so flat-out exhausted and panting at the finish line that I could not revel in the glory of a job done well or even enjoy the treat of a spa day I subsequently rewarded myself with, something I should have been doing for myself on a regular basis anyway.

Why wasn't I happy?

Hadn't I accomplished my goal?

Hadn't I pleased my bosses?

Yes. But deep down I resented myself for not having the courage to step forward and ask for what I needed. For weeks I quietly chided myself for suppressing my voice and relinquishing the choice—because it is a choice—to be heard. I am by nature an optimistic and upbeat person. But so strong was that damp feeling of discontent, it temporarily chilled my natural vibe.

By not acting in my own best interest, I had disrespected myself. I had not acted as my own advocate. What's worse, I didn't recognize the self-defeating behavior until it was too late. And that did not sit well with me. So I promised myself that it would not happen again. And it didn't.

So what made me eventually see that it's OK to ask?

I Spied on the Guys

Once I regained my energy and got my bearings back, I returned to my job as an undercover observer. I decided to watch my male counterparts and study how they approached the whole business of asking. I wanted to see them in action. What I observed made me change my own approach forever.

I saw them take their assignments, return to their boss's office, and nonchalantly present their need for a bigger budget, more resources, or extended time. I watched their body language and detected little that suggested the presence of angst. Sometimes they'd even lean against the doorjamb with their hands shoved in their pockets as they made their pitch. Based on the lack of circles under their eyes, I knew they had not lost a single night's sleep over asking. They didn't seem terribly concerned about how they'd be perceived for requesting additional resources or more time. And they wasted no energy in damaging self-editing. They weren't the least bit interested in killing themselves the way I had in order to build an island of self-sufficiency.

What I Learned

I learned that people hire you because they expect you to think critically and get things done. Yes, you need to execute, but that doesn't mean you're expected to get it done all on your own. It's perfectly acceptable to source help from other members of your team or other departments with different expertise.

What's not acceptable is playing hero for the wrong reasons. When I completed that mammoth project, I was not lauded in a proverbial parade with streaming confetti and marching bands. In fact, there was not even a passing comment about our coming in under budget. Not one. Instead of feeling proud, I felt foolish.

That's when I had a heart-to-heart with myself.

The truth was I had worried that I would be seen as weak if I asked for some tweaks to the parameters. Even worse, I was hoping that my boss would see through the situation and say something so that I wouldn't have to.

But the reality was that my poor boss had no way of knowing what I needed. He saw *me* as the expert. As the expert, it was up to me to tell him where the project needed support. He therefore—and rightfully—assumed that if there was a problem, I'd speak up. Because that's what leaders do.

The Informed Ask

What I should have done in the scenario above was analyze the situation at hand. I should have asked myself:

- How long will the project take with the current resources?

- How long would it take with more?

- What is the cost associated with finishing it sooner than later?

- What would the cost of the additional resources be?

- Without additional resources will there be overtime?

- How will that impact the budget?

Armed with the right information, you should have the confidence to ask your superiors for more time, money, or technology—whatever it is you need. Even if the answer is no, you will be perceived as having done your homework. If done properly and with a positive attitude, you won't be viewed as a whiner or complainer. Rather, your superiors will see you as fully versed in the facts and therefore capable of making a cogent request in quintessential leadership style.

More importantly, you will see yourself as a true leader. Someone with courage and grit.

Apparently Not All That Transparent

The male colleagues I observed knew the secret: The only person who can read your mind is you.

Many of us women think others should know magically what we want or need. They should see that we are overburdened, undercompensated, or stressed. And then, to top it off, we expect them to remedy the situation without our having to ask.

Think of how it goes when you are preparing a meal for a gathering of people. The timers are beeping, the dog is barking, the guests are arriving, and you still haven't washed the pots now piled high in the sink. Meanwhile, your partner or child or roomie is glued to the television, oblivious to the situation. You shoot exasperated glares at them, expecting that they'll see that you're frazzled, notice the chaos, and offer help. But no offer comes. And then you get angry. Eventually you let them know, fumes coming out of your ears, that you're in desperate need of a hand. And now they're thinking, "Well, why didn't you say something sooner?"

It's OK to Need Help

As women, we must rethink the whole topic of what it means to need help. Needing something is not the same as being needy, just as acting in one's best interest is not a negative. Speaking up for what we have accomplished is essential to garnering recognition and influence and attaining those elusive leadership positions. Asking for what we must have to sustain this level of accomplishment is not impolite, and we have to shed the notion that it is. We must shift our focus away from the potential—or perceived—feelings of those around us.

It's Not Personal

Where did we get the idea that asking for more money, responsibility, tenure, or flexibility is going to hurt someone else's feelings? Why do we think that this is an imposition to be avoided at all costs? And what's the worst that can happen? If they say no—and maybe the budget really can't accommodate your request at the moment—you are no worse off than you were before.

But maybe, just maybe, they'll say yes, and you'll be significantly better off. Either way, by stating your request, even if for the record, you'll be sending the message that you're aware of your worth. Therefore, they should be too.

He Asked

Such was the case when one of the folks working for me came across a hurdle while pursuing his master's degree. When "Tom" realized that he would have to take a class once a week in the middle of the workday, he immediately approached me with the issue. Together, we worked out an arrangement whereby he would go to his class as needed and make it up to the company by either coming in earlier or staying later for the same amount of hours. In the end, not only did he achieve his personal goal, but the company gained a more educated employee. Even better, by accommodating his request I was able to get a true commitment from him. And a commitment is always going to be better than mere compliance any day of the week.

Business Unusual

While we recognize that we women can be our own worst enemy, this does not suggest that we are imagining things, either.

There is no question that, by the time little girls grow up and make it to the boardroom, the effects of gender socialization are in full swing. We sense this, for example, when we are asking tough questions or making statements that contradict someone else's.

In my own corporate experience, I have seen firsthand how women's voices sometimes get drowned out or overlooked in meetings—including, of all things, leadership meetings. As head-scratching as it sounds, it's true. This kind of culture is still thriving in 2018.

At one company in particular, I would often find myself walking out of the room at the end of a meeting in a state of complete bewilderment. I was not alone. My small band of female colleagues would also be equally puzzled. How was it that the suggestions we had made—the very ones that were immediately ignored or glossed over—were suddenly seen as brilliant once they were revived and repackaged by a male counterpart? Were we missing something that was obvious to everyone but us? Were we misreading the scenario? Were we not using the right language? What was going on?

It got so bad that eventually the four of us—all intelligent, clear-thinking, highly educated women—actually began trying to locate the error that led to our "poor execution." Before long, we began feeling like we weren't worth the paper our diplomas had been printed on. Once alone, we talked about it quietly:

"Was it a silly suggestion?"
"Did we not say it correctly?"
"Were we being ambiguous?"
"Why did no one pick it up when we said it?"

"How was it that our male colleague could swoop down and scoop it up as if we'd just left him a tasty morsel?"

The snubs were that blatant. But once we understood that we had fallen prey to the old gender bias, we quickly shook off our denial and focused on our goals. We were determined to reestablish our position in the game. We were all experts in our fields and knew our turf. And we had worked too hard to be unceremoniously benched.

One day, we decided that we weren't having it.

The Intercept

Since we knew we couldn't change the sport, we decided to change the play. The best way to do that, we decided, was to get together ahead of the main event to practice how we would help each other win—to be heard in those meetings.

First, we looked at the agenda and decided what our contribution would be. Then we orchestrated each step. One of us would kick the idea forward. The next in line on our team would catch it and add her supporting comment. After our number two tossed it out there, the third on our team would then grab it and run, keeping the suggestion in play. By the time our fourth player caught it, no one in that room could simply ignore our contribution as if it had never been mentioned without appearing downright deaf. Even better, they could not claim it as their own without appearing utterly ridiculous or sleazy.

Our game plan worked.

While we were not heard when speaking alone, once we pulled our voices together, no one's words fell flat. I can see the furrowed foreheads in my audience now as you're reading this. You're thinking that the need to formulate such a game play should not have existed in the first place. And you're right. But the fact of the matter is, it did. And while you might be tempted to say that we should have called out the bias at the meeting right then and there, let me suggest that you never want to embarrass colleagues in the workplace by putting them on the defensive. Even if you're in the right, you'll lose. You need to apply restraint and diplomacy at all times. We decided on a smarter approach. Instead of complaining about it or, worse, capitulating, we banded together and changed the script.

Making It a Habit

Stating your case and making yourself heard is a life skill.

If you're like most women, this does not come naturally. The good news is you can develop this ability. Just as you lift weights to build muscle, you can practice speaking up. With time, consistency, and persistence, you can do it.

Put yourself in training as I did my students. Make it a game. Set goals to practice weekly or daily. Ever since that life-changing project that had me wearing a cape, I have forced myself to ask for something several times a week to keep from getting rusty. I don't ever want to be that girl again.

Today I'm in my midfifties and have over twenty-eight years' experience in the corporate world. Despite this, I still hesitate now and then when I want to ask for something huge. I still feel that tightening of the throat as I prepare to say the words. But now I put on a smile, step into that discomfort zone, and ask anyway.

The lure of silencing yourself for comfort's sake is a deep, relentless trap. Don't fall into it. Know your worth. Breathe. Open your mouth. Ask for what you want.

5

FACING FAILURE

("One stumble and it's over. I just know it.")

For years—decades, in fact—I had a fear of writing. I was convinced that anything I wrote would be prime shredder food.

This particular seed of doubt was sown when I was a twenty-year-old finance major. Taking a creative writing course to broaden my scope of skills and exposure, I was told by my professor four weeks into the course that my work was, and I quote, "no good." Without questioning his opinion or asking him to expound on it, I accepted his assessment because he was in a position of power. In that moment, I built a mental wall between a doctorate and me. I told myself that any attempt at such a lofty goal would surely end in failure.

Fast-forward to 2000. Now at J.P. Morgan as their vice president in charge of executive development, I am in my late thirties and enjoying the journey on which my career has taken me. I've even met a really nice guy, my future husband, whom I've been dating for a short while. Life is feeling like that first sip of morning coffee. But I know I want more. There is so much I want to do. And so I begin to peer longingly over the brim of my cup.

One day, I am having lunch with a colleague I have become friendly with, along with another very close mutual colleague and friend. The former, who is in the middle of pursuing her doctorate at Columbia, fills us in on her progress at my prodding. After she brings us up to date, I gush with admiration over her endeavors. When they ask why I haven't started my doctorate, I give them an apologetic, no-not-me smile and tell them that I'm not likely to be accepted by the program since my writing is not Ivy League strong.

At that point they look at me as if I've just said that exercising is bad for your health. "What?? Of course you'll get in!" they insist. "We've seen your work, Lisa. Where is all this coming from?"

I try to sell them the creative writing-course story, but they only shake their heads, completely unimpressed. "No, you're going to apply." They ignore my protests and give me a deadline to complete the application within the month. Once I have done this, they send it in for me because they don't trust that I'll actually do it.

Within four months I have my acceptance letter in my hand.

A year later I'm standing outside a building that looks as if it's been plucked out of a history book—a stoic sentry that has seen much in its time. Its weatherworn red brick, lead-framed glass windows, and grand steps leading to the heavy front door come together to present an imposing figure. I stop for a moment as we scrutinize each other. It is my first day of class. I imagine being called into the administrator's office by the end of the day because they've found out that I don't belong here. "We're so sorry," they'll say, "but we made a mistake."

Once inside, I am met with that distinct scent that old colleges have—centuries of wisdom and learning infused with the oils so faithfully applied to the dark wood. I climb the staircase with my hand on the thick wooden rail. It is smooth to the touch, worn down by the generations of students who came through these halls before me. Reaching for air through my nostrils, I tell my mind to be still. My stomach now churning, I command my legs to move forward toward my classroom. I finally arrive at the door, step into the brightly lit room, take my rightful place, and open my book. With that, I begin pursuing my doctorate.

Months pass. One day, I am sitting in my seat as Ron Silvera, one of my professors, is handing back a graded assignment—the first extensive paper since the program began. As he hands me mine, my eyes zoom to the top where he's scribbled a note: "This is brilliant work. Your writing is fantastic."

Tears begin to pool in my eyes, and I swiftly wipe them away before they're detected. But it's too late. Professor Silvera calls me up after class and asks if I'm all right. I have no choice but to share the story of my creative class. Now it's his turn to look at me as if I've spoken rubbish. "Nooo . . . " he says, "you're a good writer." And in one fell swoop, the twenty-two years of fearing failure that has been bottled up inside me vanish.

And then I wonder, "Why did I even let the fear take root to begin with? Why did I allow one person's opinion to matter?"

What Are We Really Afraid Of?

Like so many women, I made the classic mistake of accepting someone's opinion of me as fact. In my case, this was just one individual. One.

No doubt, I let my youth and position as a student goad me into capitulating. But, today, with what I now know, I wish I had had the courage to say to myself, "No, this professor doesn't get to dismiss me just like that." I wish I had had the courage to go to him and ask him—respectfully, of course—to expound on that sweeping statement. I should have asked him to defend his opinion. I'll never know what results such a conversation would have yielded, but I am willing to bet that it could have been constructive. But all is not lost. I have learned an important lesson: *Never let others define you.*

But the real issue is much simpler. What would have been the real catastrophe had I failed to produce an A paper? So what if I'd needed to work on a shaky start to a project? The way I see it, not trying at all is worse than trying and failing. What do we think is going to happen if we fail? When do we begin to be conscious of failure? And why do women shy away from it more than men?

There Once was a Wide-Eyed Little Girl

There is nothing more formidable than little girls, particularly when they're between the ages of six and eight. Ask them at that age what they want to be and they'll tell you doctor, engineer, astronaut, and, yes, president. They'll run up against any boy any ole day and take their place ruling the world. How I wish I could bottle up that essence of fearlessness and preserve it for them for when it all changes. Because, more often than not, change it does.

Once they turn ten, eleven, twelve, something happens. Suddenly, they become conscious of their bodies. They wonder if they look good in that new outfit or how they can look like the hottest celebrities. The media taunts them with suggestions that they need to be thinner, prettier, wear their hair this way and that, and fix their eyebrows and eyelashes a certain way. No longer is the universe a massive catalog. Now, it's a tiny pamphlet.

Could the problem be that we've been raised to think we have to be perfect? Is it that we've been taught that in order to have the perfect life, we have to have the perfect hair, body, SAT scores, social life, and, of course, the perfect job? Take note: when perfection is deemed the only acceptable outcome, the first casualty is our confidence.

How the Fear of Failing Affects Us

While the pursuit of perfection may be fodder for another discussion, the flip side of that—the fear of failing—can have a negative, even paralyzing, effect on women. This is because we tend to internalize it.

The consequences of avoiding failure can be profound: missed promotion opportunities, relegation to performing repetitive tasks, failure to reach personal goals, or falling short of individual potential. And in a world in which instant gratification rules, wise are the young people who try again and again and again. Each round in the ring brings them that much closer to mental fortitude.

Let's be honest. No one wants to fail. No one sets out to blunder and fall. It's how we respond and what we do when we're flat on our face that's important. And until we come to terms with the fact that failing at something (*you* are not a failure) is OK, even beneficial, women will continue to be tentative.

Studies show that from an early age, girls internalize criticism, seeing failure in a deeply personal way, while boys tend to associate mistakes with lack of effort. This tendency to depersonalize failure serves boys well later down the line.

A Bad Move

In the middle of what had been a strong and steady climb in my career, I made what would be a not-so-great decision to change my job for one in another state. While the new position was challenging, the culture ended up being an uncomfortable fit for me—one I knew would eat away at my soul. Within days of settling into my new office, I felt the air growing thick. I had found myself in an environment I could not survive in. To make it worse, I could only go home on weekends. I began to struggle just to get out of bed each morning. My prayers to God became longer as I put myself in His hands. I needed Him to tell me what to do.

With no parachute or plan B, I packed my bags and left after only six months, the tapes in my head already playing the *What Will People Say* soundtrack as I gathered the last of my belongings on my final day. Without even giving myself a chance, I immediately labeled the whole experience (cue dramatic organ music) a failure.

Never before had I been in this position. Worse, I had broken one of my cardinal rules about not burning bridges. But even golden rules have caveats. In this case, this was one bridge simply not meant for me to take. And yet, despite knowing this, I couldn't see the experience for what it was: a simple wrong turn.

For the longest while, I binged on self-flagellation for what I perceived as a major misstep. God bless my husband. No matter how many times I replayed the details with him, Carl listened while giving me his full attention, not once cutting me off, sighing, or glancing at the television remote control. Then one day, while I was in the middle of yet another soliloquy, he finally stopped me.

"Lisa, why are you doing this? Why are you taking this all out on yourself like it's your fault? I'm kinda surprised at you, actually. Us men, we just don't do that."

They don't?

A Better Way

Carl was right, of course. Men by and large think nothing of brushing off a disappointment such as this like lint on their sleeve. ("Yeah, whatever. Next!") Not us. We tend to obsess over it as if it were a giant stain we won't ever get out.

We need to take a cue from our male counterparts on this one. How powerful and liberating it would be if more women embraced the idea that failure is one of several possible by-products of courage—the courage to go out there and try. We need to see that failure is not a referendum on our capabilities. Nor should fear of success be a barrier: "What if I actually get that promotion and *can't* do the job?" How many times have we whispered that one to ourselves?

There are numerous examples of everyday products that resulted from failures—from chocolate chip cookies to sticky notepaper—and yet many of us women shy away from taking chances. We can ponder all day what the root causes of this fear might be. It's more important, however, to acknowledge the opportunity costs of playing it safe and its potential to derail careers. Once you've done that, identify ways to get past the fear of failure.

As for my personal PS, once I woke up and saw my "failure" as just another reminder to take every experience as a lesson, I returned to the consultancy business I had started earlier, breathed new energy into it, and renewed the confidence in myself that I had lost. And when word got around at my church that I had left the job, one of the church elders came up to me one Sunday and gave me the biggest smile. "We were praying you home every day, Lisa," she said. "It took Him a little while, but eventually God heard us."

I am grateful for the misstep that took me temporarily off course. Had it not happened, I might not be where I am today. Not only did it make me more aware of what I don't want, but it refueled my passion for the things that I do. Now when I look at my life's mosaic, I see this unhappy experience as a mere blip in what is an otherwise incredibly pleasing work of art.

The Role of Social Media

The generation of young women in the workplace today grew up in a world of instant messages and social media that took them from Myspace to Facebook to Instagram to Twitter to Tumblr. Their lives have been led in full view of "friends" and "followers," and measured by likes.

Blogging and sharing (not to mention oversharing) is an inextricable part of their everyday lives. The price of failing, therefore, is perhaps higher than it used to be. Years ago, if you made a mistake, you would sulk alone in your room, recover at your own pace, dust yourself off, and move on. With the exception of a few close friends, perhaps, you pretty much had the entire movie theater of failure to yourself.

Today, the implications are different, with a person's failure often taking place in full view of others. Failure (or perceived failure) is now in the public domain. Boyfriend break up with you? (Translation: failed relationship.) He changes his status from "in a relationship with . . . " to "single." In an instant, your 1,437 friends know that you've been dumped. Got laid off? How many people get an email when your LinkedIn profile changes? "Congratulate Betty on her new job!" Maybe her new job is a placeholder for no job. No wonder that the stakes are higher and women feel more vulnerable. All this may lead some women to take fewer risks. Privacy standards have all but vanished. The chance to lick one's wounds without the world watching is nearly nonexistent. For those of us born in the pre-Internet era, this brings new meaning to the phrase "the good old days."

Pressure from Within

Another potential factor here is the fact that many of the young women in the workforce were raised by bright, well-educated mothers who themselves were ambitious women.

In earlier generations, many girls were raised by more traditional June Cleaver-like stay-at-home moms who may or may not have been educated. While today's young women may not have been raised by full-out tiger moms (moms who practice traditional, strict child-rearing with exceedingly high standards and no tolerance for second best), they may have had parents who were so invested in their success that there was no room for anything short of it. There was no tolerance for failure in the classroom, in the concert hall, or on the field. It's no wonder, then, that these young women feel such pressure. It's the only environment many of them have ever known.

Valuable Lessons

Too many children, girls especially, want desperately to please. Failing at something pleases no one, it seems. But is that the right takeaway? While it's always good to get something right (we all want that), I guarantee that you have the opportunity to learn a whole lot more when you get something wrong. And this makes perfect sense if you think about it.

For example: You are doing budget projections and discover that you are off the mark. What steps might you take? You revisit your assumptions and trace back to what didn't add up. This more granular analysis leads to a deeper understanding of all the individual pieces that go into that budget. Ask yourself:

- What trends did you miss?

- What factors led to stronger- or weaker-than-anticipated orders?

- What factors might have contributed to the different results? Were costs higher or lower than anticipated?

This data mining brings you much closer to your core business and makes you an expert in the next round of budget projections.

Sure, you came up short in one round, but it's all about what you learn and how you apply it going forward.

When I failed at an ill-prepared presentation while still relatively young in the corporate world, I admit to wasting two whole weeks nursing my wounds. It took a visit to my tough-love mentor, Toby (more on her and mentoring in chapter 9), to yank me out of my pity party.

"Of course you're not a total disaster! That's *shitsky* talk," she said, using her signature Brooklyn street slang. "I know you won't let it happen again. So get over it by getting something out of it."

Toby was right. I could still examine the disaster site and use it as an opportunity to learn. And so I took an honest look at my performance. I asked myself:

- What did I feel?

- What went well?

- How did I miss the mark?

- What were the various reactions?

- How could I have done this better or differently?

I now apply this overview to as many situations as I can, from a one-on-one meeting that didn't quite produce the results I had hoped for to a major client presentation. The objective is to learn. In the case of making presentations such as the one that fell flat, if I had friends in the audience or meeting, I ask them for their perspectives, too. I seek their feedback.

Feedback: Free, Priceless

I am big on feedback, yet it's something that women generally don't get or ask for. But if you want to develop a strong mental attitude, you have no choice here. You must get into the habit of getting into that arena. I know you're saying, "Easier said than done, Lisa!" Yes, I know. It can be messy work. But sweating is good for you.

I once saw a male boss give feedback to the female employee on his team. Shifting in his chair, angst all over his face, I knew he was not happy. When I asked him about it, he admitted that his hesitation stemmed from the fact that she would often cry when confronted with criticism. Not knowing what to do, he eventually stopped. But I told him to continue doing his job, because she could only improve through his input.

"Neither of you wins this way," I said. "Not only is it your job to offer constructive criticism, but you also can't allow tears, whether real or rehearsed, to sabotage progress."

I admit that my first exposure to criticism was at the hands of a master "boss"—my father. He knew how to deliver criticism without crushing my spirit. I remember back when I was still learning cursive writing. Still struggling at the hot-mess stage, I showed him my first attempt.

"Well," he said with a fatherly nod, "I'm certainly proud of you for your effort. But how about trying again and seeing if you can improve on that a little?"

If you are in the position of critiquing others, be mindful of your tone and words. I'm not suggesting that you coddle. That's also destructive. But while some will rise above tough words, there's still no need to be cruel and demeaning.

Are Tears on the Job OK?

We are all given to having emotion in some way, even when on the job. That's what makes us human. The challenge is that the standards differ based on gender. It is generally accepted that a man can show his frustrations by raising his voice, cursing, throwing things around, or pounding his fist on the desk. But if a woman so much as lets her lips tremble, she's labeled as weak. And yet she's simply displaying a human emotion like any other.

If you're a leader, you need to be able to handle emotion from subordinates. But what if you're the woman in the leadership position whose eyes are about to well up because you've just been told something that deeply moves or upsets you? Does your position as head honcho preclude you from bringing your whole self to the table? Do you wait until you're alone in your office, ask your secretary to hold all calls, and then let it out?

Let's be honest and talk about the optics of it all. Tears can be controversial. And each situation is different. What is interpreted as weakness in a more formal industry may find more latitude in another. Like it or not, women are wired differently from men. That's just how our DNA works. The point is to take a deep breath and be aware.

Facing Criticism with Grace

As women, we probably do need to practice harder at taking criticism with a smile. No one likes to hear they're performing poorly. But if you're going to improve, you need to know what to work on. Here are some ways to take criticism like a champ:

- Assume good intent on the part of the person giving the criticism.

- Listen then ask questions calmly, without being defensive.

- Ask for specific examples if you don't understand.

- Be gracious. The person is giving you their time and expertise.

- Show gratitude for the investment being made in you by learning.

Sometimes, however, feedback is not accurate. If it feels completely off, seek a second opinion from someone you respect and ask them to be honest with you. Ask them if it rings true. In fact, ask them how they see you in general. Find out how they rate you in the following categories:

- Approachability
- Confidence
- Reliability
- Self-awareness
- Temperament
- Work ethic

Whatever the response, decide that you will use the information as fire that forges steel.

Grab a Mirror (and More Pen and Paper)

Not to be forgotten is your own opinion. If you can get into that honest place with yourself, you could well be the source of the most influential feedback, period. I now make it a habit to assess myself at the end of each week by carrying out my own after-action review for events large and small. Try it for a month and see what you learn.

- Write the name of the event(s) at the top of a sheet of paper. Draw a line underneath it.

- Draw a line down the middle of the page to create two columns below with a + sign on the left for the things that went well, and a – sign for the things that could have been better.

- Be honest in your assessment. Make it a point to change what didn't work (e.g., execution, attention to detail) and double down on what did (e.g., energy, teamwork).

The Compliment Barometer

Criticism isn't the only feedback you'll receive, though. Brace yourself for the flurry of praise and kudos that will come your way. How do you take compliments? Do you smile and thank the person for taking the time to acknowledge your effort? Or do you disrespect it with a negative comeback?

If you're guilty of the latter, stop now. Nothing is more of a turnoff than when someone rejects what is usually a genuine compliment. Someone saw it fit to honor you with their time and observation. When you reject that observation, you reject them. Playing coy is unattractive in this scenario. But if it's the case that you truly feel unworthy of the kind words, then it might be an indication that you're running low on self-worth. Time to fill up on feel-good fuel. Hack your way to self-confidence until you no longer need to fake it. In the meantime, smile and say, "Thank you."

You're Gonna Pay for This

The real takeaway message is that tentativeness—lack of confidence—is not without cost. Creativity suffers—and the what-ifs begin to pile up.

Innovation implies failure. And yet few new ideas work on the first iteration. We already know about the confidence gap between men and women. What this means is that women may not offer an idea or suggestion at a meeting for fear that it's not good enough. Or they may be less likely to take a stretch assignment if they lack confidence in their ability to succeed.

In my own practice, I've seen men apply for jobs for which they know they are, at best, only 60 percent qualified. Not so with my female clients. If there are ten skill sets needed for a certain position, chances are they won't even apply unless they have at least eight or nine. Meanwhile, their male counterparts have already sent in their applications and résumés because they assume they're a shoo-in. This happens, I regret to say, more than we realize.

Reframe That Picture

When I work with female clients who are trying to get past something they "failed" at, I get them to reframe their perspective.

- I start by having them change the language they use about themselves, most of which is internalized. If they joke about a perceived general lack of ability (e.g., "I was born without the math gene."), I remind them that the brain can't distinguish between a joke and fact.

- I suggest that perhaps a project failed in the past because the team they were working with wasn't ready for that particular approach. Maybe they were intimidated by the drastic change in thinking.

- I tell them to see their past failure as a stepping-stone. Had that failure not happened, they would not be where they are now. You could argue that they could have gotten there without it, but would they have arrived with the same level of gratitude and commitment? Thanks to the experience along the road, they now know what they want and don't want.

As Katty Kay and Claire Shipman point out in their book *The Confidence Code*, "success correlates more closely with confidence than it does with competence." Joyce Ehrlinger, a Washington State University psychologist, noted in one of her studies that "because [women] are less confident in general in their abilities, that led them not to want to pursue future opportunities."

Kay and Shipman go on to observe that, "many girls learn to avoid taking risks and making mistakes. This is to their detriment. Many psychologists now believe that risk taking, failure, and perseverance are essential to confidence-building."

Turning Setbacks into Strength

Sara Blakely, founder of Spanx and the youngest self-made female billionaire in history, insists that her success resulted from her father's staunch belief in the power of "failing big."

In her interview with *Business Insider* publication in 2016, she recalls childhood dinner-table conversations that began with her father asking her what she had failed at that day. In this way, her father encouraged her to try things outside her comfort zone and to feel safe if she failed. He was sending her the message that failing was nothing to be ashamed of. More importantly, the dinner ritual taught a young Sara to resist attaching failure to an outcome and to connect it instead to an attempt to be more than she was the day before. And as we know from her famous success story, failure worked well for her. If she hadn't failed the LSAT exam, she would have become a lawyer and never would have invented Spanx. And if she hadn't done that, she wouldn't have become the trailblazing entrepreneur she is today.

Accepting failure as part of our personal learning continuum is liberating. Not only are failures the arcs of our lives that shape us, but they are, I would argue, the precursors to true innovation and personal growth.

Following Katie Couric's first on-air television experience, which by her own admission was "horrible," the head of CNN called the assignment desk and said he never wanted to see her on the air again. According to Couric in an interview with Andrew Goldman of *The New York Times*, that devastating experience "forced me to get better." And that's exactly what she did. Not only is perfection unrealistic, but it is sometimes undesirable.

Break free from that perfectionist mind-set. There is no shame in feeling fear—we all do at some point. Even the big, strong, strapping guys do. But we have to push through, even if it means finding out in the end that we don't like the end goal.

For me, this habit of commitment—once again—was instilled in me by my parents, and particularly my mom. My sister-in-law pointed out the great gift she had given us at one of our family gatherings. "My parents let my siblings and me quit things all the time," she said. "We liked that when we were kids, of course. But little did we know that that was going to hurt us in the long run. Your mom never let you guys get away with that. I don't know if you even realize it, but that life lesson was pure gold."

Finishing What You Start

My sister-in-law was absolutely right, of course. Anne knew exactly what she was teaching her children when she insisted that we finished whatever we started. It is a life skill that has served me well. If this is missing in your life, it's not too late. Make a promise to cross that finish line no matter how difficult. Even if you find out after taking a three-month-long course on blogging that you really don't like it or that it was a colossal mistake, you will still have won in two ways:

1. You now know through experience that blogging is not for you. This means that you will likely not waste more time or money moving in this direction, because you've already test-driven that vehicle.

2. You have honored another commitment to yourself. Nothing eats away at your self-esteem quite like unfinished business. Do *not* become a cop-out queen. Build a life of always crossing the finish line no matter what. Even if you have to crawl or limp past it, you will still feel like a champion.

Your Fear-Challenge Fact Sheet

Write a fact sheet listing all those times in your life you stared fear in the face and plowed right through it. Nothing is too small to include. If it gave you even a moment's hesitation, it counts. For example:

CHALLENGE	FEAR FACTOR LEVEL (1–10)	RESULT
Started martial arts at age 35.	5—Learned alongside kids half my age.	Developed killer body and learned to take down grown men.
Returned to workforce after 20 years when spouse suffered stroke.	10—Had kids, growing debt, and no plan B.	Learned new skills and made it. Family grew stronger.
Confronted family member about decades-old dispute.	7—It had the potential to make the rift worse.	Issue still unresolved, but debilitating inertia ended once I spoke my truth.
Walked into new French bakery over the weekend.	4—Had not had any refined sugar for a whole month.	Stuck to diet. Walked out of there with only coffee—no sugar added. Yay, me!
Gave toast at best friend's wedding.	10—First speech in front of large audience with strangers.	Pulled it off and didn't die.
Took online course on blogging.	7—Technology intimidates me. I grew up with typewriters.	Learned enough basics to start my own simple blog.
Spoke up in class last week.	8—I never volunteer answers unless asked by the teacher.	The class agreed with my answer. Felt amazing.
Spoke to three strangers in one week.	8—I have anxiety about approaching strangers.	Each conversation was short but pleasant.

What are *your* mountains?

Decide that you're going to face them now. Decide that you're going to climb them one by one, no matter how much cold sweat it produces and no matter how many bumps and bruises you get. Tell yourself that you won't be defeated. Remind yourself that it is through defeat that you learn who you are and what you're made of.

Challenge yourself often. Find something weekly. Be deliberate about it. Feel your pulse quicken. See yourself at the edge of your intellectual or emotional seat. Once you've programed your bio-chemistry to know this feeling, you'll remember it the next time you're faced with a bigger hurdle. And that's when you'll tell yourself that you'll make over this new one just fine.

Have faith that once you commit to doing something, your mind will automatically recruit all the mental muscles it needs. Over time, your courage will grow.

And so will your good reputation with the person who matters most: *you.*

6

RISKING EXPERIENCE TO CHANGE THE GAME

("Can't I just sail through life and wait for big things to happen for me?")

I have a secret crush on my students.

I love hearing what they're thinking about and, more importantly, what they're dreaming about. They motivate and inspire me. That said, more often than not I find myself rushing to redirect my female charges when I catch them hesitating or second-guessing their natural instincts to aim high.

"Oh, honey, no! You're not dreaming big enough!" I tell them. "Don't hold back. *Ever.*" It is a knee-jerk reaction that I'm not interested in controlling anytime soon.

Sometimes, however, I hear my tone bordering on a full-on plea. I wish I could literally grab them by the shoulders and shake them free of the social conditioning that has trained us girls to take cautious steps so that we don't trip and scar our pretty little knees.

It is at moments like these that I am reminded that, even though time has passed and much has changed, we are not yet there. We still have work to do. While we know intellectually that we deserve to be at the party, we still don't believe it. Whenever I see this in young women, I am reminded of my schoolgirl days, when my friends would dumb down their intelligence and ambitions for the sake of popularity with other girls or, even worse, to get the attention of a boy.

Ironically, it was a broken heart—caused by a boy who would not give me his attention—that drove me to take one of my first major career moves. One that, dare I say, paid off handsomely.

Running into the Open Arms of Risk

My former beau and I met in college. After five or six years of dating, once graduation was a couple years behind us, we finally broached the topic of marriage. But talking was as far as he'd take it. While he was a great guy and the relationship was equally good, the timing was, well, you know *that* story, right?

In an attempt to save my investment of time and emotion, I delivered what ended up being an ill-fated ultimatum.

Soon after, amid tears, I found myself packing my bags to take a new position in New York. My mother and a friend came to help. Mom handed me my clothes and passed me Kleenex while she sang a tough-woman anthem ("Oh please, baby girl, he did you a favor!"). My friend was her backup singer ("In fact, be sure to send him a huge thank-you card!"). Before I knew it I was off to New York while I wiped away the tears that wouldn't stop falling.

I was terrified.

I was a small-town girl. The biggest city I knew was Philadelphia. New York City was another planet to me. I just knew that I was going to be swallowed by the sea of people rushing about their lives. I prepared myself for lonely nights in my studio apartment eating Chinese takeout while sitting in front of the television. But somehow that whole lonely-in-a-big-city scenario never took root. I began to make friends and settled in.

Not long after, the opportunity of a lifetime appeared.

The telecommunications field—and particularly the wireless segment—just happened to be expanding globally at this time. It was an exciting time in the industry. While it was already burgeoning in the US, it was only now gaining traction in Europe and Asia.

One day, my colleagues and I were called into an expansion consortium meeting. The topic: entering the Greek market. The question was put to us: Who wanted to carry the company banner into that market? But all I heard was: Who wanted to go far, far away?

In what I can only describe as an out-of-body experience, my hand shot up. Much to my genuine shock, it was the only hand over a sea of heads. Adrenaline coursed through me when I realized that it was going to be me on that plane in less than two months. Literally a minute later it was confirmed. The company had called my bluff. It immediately began to make plans to send my broken heart and me to Greece.

Still numb over what I had just done, I packed up my life for a stint almost halfway across the world. I was heading to a country I had never visited, where they spoke a language I couldn't identify if I heard it on the street. I was shaking even as I caught my taxi from Athens's airport to my hotel. To calm myself, I reached for my New York experience. "You've done this before, Lisa," I said. "Breathe. You've got this."

The next day I woke up and began the countdown. But within a few weeks, I pivoted and began to see the experience as a challenge of a lifetime. Before I knew it, I was counting down again, not in my eagerness to leave but in my new wish to live out the adventure just a little longer.

Bolstered by my success, I repeated the experience twice after this. I volunteered to take our product to Jakarta (without even knowing where Indonesia was) and then did a final stint in Prague. By my early thirties, I had experienced living abroad in three amazing and incredibly different countries in three different languages and had fallen in love all over again—this time with myself and my not-so-terribly-scarred knees. Once I returned home from this life-altering experience, I felt like a retooled machine, ready to take on any challenge.

I still think back to the day I sent my hand shooting into the air for that first posting in Greece and how genuinely surprised I was to find myself alone in the desire for adventure.

Today, I understand why there weren't more takers. It is natural for us to gravitate to our comfort zones, even in our youth. We like leaning on the known and the familiar. It's safe. It's nonthreatening.

So keep close this insider tip on human nature the next time you're faced with a golden opportunity to grow. Take advantage of the fact that most individuals will hesitate before taking take that leap of faith, if they take it at all. Let that image of me in the meeting that day be a reminder that the difference between losing out and lucking out can be as simple as raising your hand.

Knowledge is Power, but Experience is the Game Changer

There's not a whole lot that a competent googler can't find out these days.

It may take a few searches, changing the key words, or phrasing it like a question, but just about everything is knowable. Whether you research your symptoms before you visit the doctor, look into your boss's or colleague's background, or find the perfect chimichurri sauce recipe to match the one you had at the restaurant last night, you can find anything.

The reality, however, is that in today's world, having knowledge no longer makes you special. It doesn't put you in a category that stands out. The problem is that for many people, once they feel empowered with facts and figures, they stop there.

Today, knowledge is only part of the story. Research, analysis, and a command of the facts are imperative. But knowledge without experience is one-dimensional. True empowerment, therefore, springs from experience.

Some people are daunted by the old conundrum "I can't get a job without experience, and I can't get experience because I don't have a job." There's obviously some truth in that—especially for new college graduates. But the good news is that experience comes in lots of forms.

So if you really, *really* want it, you can have it.

Wheels Up

When fighter pilots take to the skies to do battle, they do so knowing they won't have the luxury of circling back down when they're running out of fuel. Instead, they refuel in midair, right in the middle of the action. That's how they keep on going.

We need to have the same attitude when it comes to our goals: barrel down that runway and take off. Pretty simple advice on the surface, but it can be much more difficult for those who suffer from analysis paralysis.

You know who you are.

You analyze and overanalyze and then analyze again before making a move—*if* you make one at all. I'm all for informed decision-making and gathering the relevant facts before committing to something, but there are times when you need to close your eyes, count backward from three, and do it before you change your mind. You may not have all the facts. You may not even be right. But making a decision, acting on it, and finding out sooner rather than later whether it was right or wrong beats inertia every time.

Be brave. Say yes to something that scares you.

Not long ago, I asked my students in their first week of class the question that motivational speakers have been provoking their audiences with for years now: What one thing would you dare to do if you knew you could not fail?

Not one hand went up.

"First thought!" I urged. "Don't overthink. Just spit it out."

Nothing. Not one of the thirty-five hands appeared. Worse, their faces froze as if facing a firing squadron.

My heart sank.

If there's someone in your life you care deeply about, ask them this question. Even if they can't answer immediately, it will at least nudge them to look inside themselves and become accountable.

This is another way of saying, "Tell me who you are."

I love stretching myself. I am the first to admit that, more often than not, I have had to talk myself away from the edge. Nothing brings color to my cheeks quite like making myself take a healthy risk. That said, I won't bet the whole farm, either. I'll examine all sides of it with patience and logic. And even though I'm an optimist, I'll take a look at the worst-case scenario for good measure.

But once I make my peace with the latter, once I can accept it, I will picture myself landing on both feet, regardless of the outcome. I'm not advocating that everyone go jump off the proverbial cliff tomorrow, but there are often opportunities—both in and out of the workplace—to experience something new by just raising your hand, especially when it's out of your comfort zone. In fact, I'd even suggest that if you're feeling a little too comfortable and are operating by rote, then it may be time to strap in and head for the skies.

Small Steps. Significant Returns.

But let's put aside references to cliffs and the like. You'd be surprised at how even just a small step in the right direction can lead to something huge. For example, when you're in a meeting that is wrapping up and the leader is doling out action items, throw your hat in the ring. It could be as easy as:

- Distributing notes you've taken

- Building a useful PowerPoint deck

- Contacting others about joining the project

- Conducting follow-up research without being asked

Grab experience by the arm even if it brings on a case of nervous jitters. Get to know new people in your organization. Learn a new skill. Really put yourself out there. And don't wait to feel sure about it. If you need help, ask for it (hopefully you didn't skip chapter 4). Even that simple act shows others that you are engaged, brave, curious, eager to learn, and able to take initiative—all qualities that leaders demonstrate.

Some companies even offer secondments—opportunities to temporarily change roles and/or locations within the organization. This could offer a wonderful, relatively risk-free way to gain experience in another functional area or in another region of the world. Look around you. What opportunities do you see? Use them wisely, and they'll make you an attractive candidate with real potential for advancement.

Which leads directly to my next point: it's good to get your hands dirty.

Rolling Up Your Sleeves

This can mean a lot of things at different places, but the idea is that you should always welcome the opportunity to dig beneath the surface.

In some workplaces, that might mean looking at empirical data. Elsewhere, it might mean familiarizing yourself with processes or taking on some menial but important task that will lead to a deeper understanding of how the whole enterprise functions. Today, you don't hear about too many CEOs who started in the mailroom, but there is a definite advantage for those who are willing to put in the effort to learn the operation from the inside out. Ursula Burns, the former CEO and chairman of Xerox, is just one such example. From the time she began at Xerox in 1980 as a summer intern, her rise to the top was filled with examples of her gathering experience at every turn. The value of experience cannot be overstated—you are the sum total of what you have done, seen, produced, created, explored, tried, failed at, and succeeded at. It all adds up to one thing: *experience.*

Beyond the Workplace

OK, so you don't feel like there are opportunities to get experience outside your role where you work. For whatever reason—the culture, your department, your boss—you don't feel like you can ask for experience outside your function. What then?

Take a broader view.

Look beyond your workplace and volunteer strategically. This might sound cynical to some, but if you are looking to gain experience doing X, find a nonprofit that needs someone to do just that and volunteer your time. It can only be a win-win. You get to try something new and acquire a new skill, and the organization benefits because someone has stepped up to fill the role. There are some wonderful websites where you can search for local volunteer opportunities (www.idealist.org and www.volunteermatch.org are two great resources). Want to move into a communications role but don't have experience? Volunteer to write the newsletter at a charity of your choice. Looking for a switch to the finance department? Volunteer to be the treasurer at your local garden club or YMCA. Thinking of moving into a leadership role? Teach or mentor at a children's sports club or nonprofit organization or go for the position of PTA president.

These types of roles allow you to say, "I did that" or "I did something similar to that." Remember, too, that what you choose to do for free speaks volumes about how you feel—what you're passionate about. These volunteer posts can only enhance both your résumé and personal brand.

And don't forget to connect the dots. By this, I mean the experiences that you have already accumulated in other areas of your life: in your sorority. At your church. At your summer camp.

Even past hurdles in your personal life show a potential employer what you're really made of. Perhaps you overcame a serious illness that changed your life. Lost a lot of weight and completely transformed your body. Survived bullying or an abusive relationship and grew stronger.

When my father died suddenly, leaving behind his young family, my mother swallowed her tears and changed jobs temporarily for more financial stability. She left her teaching job and went to work in a factory where the pay was better. In this case, she didn't take on the experience to further her career but to improve her situation. More than supporting her family, however, the experience taught her that she could think, act decisively, and survive no matter what. As a result, she won the admiration and respect not just of others but also of herself.

I, too, can draw from this experience of losing a family member.

That April day, I had just come home from school when my mom asked me to come sit with her. She had something to tell me, she said. Even today I can still see myself in my yellow short-sleeved dress, white knee socks, and brown loafers, my hair in pigtails. My brother was at a football practice, so it was just the two of us in the house. When she said the words—when she told me that my father had gone—I stared at her with a sense of disbelief and confusion. I leaned forward and let my body slump into her arms. We sat there for the longest while in a tight, quiet huddle.

In the days and weeks that followed, a sense of resilience rose above the deep sadness that fell upon our household. We held it together. Missing school was not an option. Nor was dropping out of our other activities. It was still hard, of course. And as this was our first experience with tragedy, we were learning as we went along. Sometimes I'd catch Mom looking wistfully out of the window. In her attempt to be strong for us, she never let us see her cry. But even at that age, I sensed her loneliness and anxiety. So I decided to be strong for her, too. When I didn't have the words to comfort her, I'd snuggle against her as if to tell her that I was there and that it was going to be all right. We stuck together, our small band, including our dog, Skippy. From our loss, and from this experience, I got the message that I had to be able to take care of myself no matter what.

Draw connections and make references to how you perceived or handled situations. These experiences need not be tragic to make an impact. Maybe you served on a Greek life council at your university, where each sorority and fraternity had different ideas of how things should run. Maybe you were able to build consensus or observed someone else skillfully bridging gaps between different viewpoints and learned from it. Whatever it is and whichever area it's from—life, work, family, sports—use it. It is *real* experience, and it counts. And you bring all of it with you in every situation.

Remember that you're a package. Take a peek inside now and then. Appreciate the gift that you are.

Getting out There

Of course, all of this implies engaging life and really putting yourself out there. Be willing to make mistakes in order to grow. Ask questions. Yes, be vulnerable. Taking a chance—a risk—can lead to a host of experiences that ultimately put you on a different path or even on the same path but at a different pace. The more you see, feel, observe, absorb, try, and analyze, the deeper the personal well you have from which to draw. But you can't fill that well without getting out there. You can't do it by sitting on the sidelines. You have to do the work.

Experience, even if indirect, can quickly morph into motivation. It may be just the thing you need to join a new conversation in the hallway or move from the sidelines to the center of the action. The bottom line is that experience is *the* game changer. Not only can it change the way people see you, but it may, more importantly, change the way you see yourself.

It happened to me.

From Side Hustle to Main Gig

When I graduated from high school, I assumed that I'd enjoy a career in finance. I was good at math and made what felt like a logical choice. I earned my undergraduate degree in financial management and embarked on a career in that field. But when I began talking to colleagues (mostly women) about their career aspirations and encouraging them to reach for more—simply because it felt natural—I began developing a reputation for being a sideline mentor.

Before long, I was hooked on helping others.

When colleagues I didn't know very well began popping into my office to ask for some time with me because they'd heard that I had helped out this person or that, I could practically feel my eyes light up. I didn't have this reaction only because I was doing something I enjoyed. I was excited because I was listening to my gut, taking chances, embracing experiences, and letting each challenge organically take me to my next logical step.

The dots were starting to connect.

Suddenly, a pathway cleared before me to suggest a potential destination that had otherwise not shown itself. Now I was motivated to carve out the real journey meant for me. Now I was seeing myself in a different light. So when I eventually decided on pursuing a master's degree in human resources, I was hardly surprised.

You Never Know Who's Watching

One day while at work on a cold February morning in 2000, I was sifting through my correspondence when I saw a letter addressed to me from the *Network Journal.* I slipped my letter opener along the side and ripped it open. Seconds later I sat back in my chair. I had been selected as one of that year's "25 Most Influential Black Women in Business."

The backstory brought more tears to my eyes than even the letter itself did. Unbeknownst to me, my name had been submitted by some of the young women I had been mentoring. When they heard about the upcoming award, they each wrote a paragraph stating why I deserved to be selected.

I had never actually set my sights on mentoring per se. I just knew that pulling out the potential in people gave me purpose. Using my talent to serve others filled me with warmth even more than that most sumptuous first-thing-in-the-morning cup of coffee. And as I consider coffee to be a core value, this should tell you something.

On the day the award was presented, I stood there marveling at the illustrious group of women that had been gathered. It occurred to me that day that we could change the nation if we pooled our powers together. *One day at a time,* I said to myself. *We will change the narrative.*

Taking the Risk in Honor of Those Who Couldn't

When the tears began to fall the day I got that letter, they were not just for myself but also for my mother. This was a moment I would have wanted to share with her. As I sat in my office alone, I let my mind drift to her and the women of her era. I thought of the many dreams they had buried in their souls. They would never get such a letter. Or such an honor.

Five years after my father's death, Mom remarried and gave us another good man as our stepfather. With a new partner to share her life with, she returned to teaching. Life settled down again for her. But when I hit my senior year of high school, my parents told me they would be moving to Hawaii once I left for college. I didn't believe them, of course. Who ups and relocates almost five thousand miles away? But that's what they did.

While at the time I was not happy about losing the only home I had ever known, my parents' massive move taught me two important lessons: One, home is not a physical place; it really is where your heart lies. Two, you do yourself and others a great honor by taking risks for the dreams that make you feel alive.

Not only did they follow through on this major decision, but Mom even learned to swim at the age of fifty-six with the Red Cross. And, just to make the journey even more poignant, she took her final certification test in a huge arena: the Pacific Ocean.

Before It's Too Late

My stepfather died twenty-two years after he married my mom.

Now an adult, I was in a better position to comfort her this time. I decided that I would spoil her a little—maybe take her traveling. This would be Anne's time now. She finally had the luxury of being able to think only of herself and no one else. She could explore her untapped dreams and write wonderful new chapters for her life.

But literally within a few months of burying her second husband, this amazing, brave woman who had sacrificed much for the sake of her children was diagnosed with terminal stomach cancer. It was discovered far too late, and there was little hope for her. This time, I was the one who got the news from the doctor.

It was the middle of the day, and I was home alone with my mom. When the phone rang, I quickly intercepted the call, grateful that she was distracted with a chore. When the doctor said the words I had been dreading, my throat tightened as my head began spinning. I could barely whisper a thank you. When the call ended, I knew I couldn't face my mom just yet. Driven by a sudden urge to collapse into the comfort of God's love, I slipped out of the house and ran to our church. For what felt like hours, I sobbed in the empty pews for the two fathers I had lost and for my mother, who now had less than a year to live. I begged God to stay by her side as she lived out her final days. I asked Him to give her as painless a transition as possible. And I begged Him to give me the strength to be the rock she needed me to be. Because in that moment, I was anything but strong.

In the months that followed, I saw my mother's rapid decline in her eyes.

The light of someone once so fierce and vibrant was now diminishing like a setting sun. It shook my faith in even gravity itself. In the hospital during her final phase, I spoke the most gut-wrenching words I have ever had to, even to this day: "Mommy, Mommy, if this is too hard for you, if you're too tired, you can go. I will be OK." As the words came out, I knew immediately that she had been waiting to hear them. Her smile, while weak, was bursting with love and relief.

I took a leave of absence from work and took her home.

It's All in Your Hands

It was fall.

With the temperature still fresh and the sky still a deep, saturated blue, Mom and I spent hours in our chaise lounges in our backyard.

When it got cool, I'd curl up next to her and throw a light blanket over us. Sometimes we'd lie there in silence. Other times we'd talk. She told me how proud she was of the woman I had become. But I knew she was worried for me. I was her baby—and her daughter.

I told her that she didn't have to worry. I told her she had worked hard to give me the gifts of a determined mind, spirit of grace, and strong wings to fly, and that she had done her job well. She squeezed my hand, the sad smile on her face saying what words could not.

But there was more. I felt it.

I thought back to my schoolgirl days when Mom would indulge me as I orchestrated Saturday-night talent shows with the neighborhood kids, and when she'd encourage me to try out for the cheerleading and field hockey teams.

She wasn't just trying to keep her child entertained. She was teaching her little girl how to take on the world—pushing her through any door she could find even when all her daughter could see was a plain wall. All the years and effort she had poured into me, all the sacrifices she had made to shore me up, were her way of passing on to me all the dreams that she had to let pass her by.

I will tell you this: while losing my mom remains the most painful part of my life, knowing that she died with her dreams still trapped inside of her is what keeps me up at night.

Years before this, a friend of mine who had just lost her mother told me that you really only grow up once your mother dies. At the time I didn't quite understand. After all, I was already a well-adjusted, full-grown adult with a job, many responsibilities, and a balanced life. But for some reason, I let her words register—locked and loaded. So when my mom took her last breath in my arms that November evening at 7:51 p.m., those words came flooding back to and through me.

To this day I can't quite describe it, except to say that I had a visceral reaction—a notion of being handed a baton by the woman who had carried me up to that point of my life. She had ended her leg of the journey at only age sixty-eight. Her time was over. Now it was up to me to carry on. I promised myself that I would take her story with me wherever I went.

When I opened that letter from the *Network Journal* in my office that day, I had just laid my mom to rest not three months before. Sitting in my office alone, my closed door temporarily cutting me off from the white noise of office life, my mind flew to her instantly. It was as if she were telling me again how proud she was of me and reminding me that life is what I choose it to be: a shallow wading pool or a deep, beautiful ocean.

I'm begging you. Raise your arms high, close your eyes, and dive in.

7

SEEKING EXPOSURE

("I don't want to be the new kid who doesn't know where the cafeteria is.")

Meet Exposure—Risk's calmer first cousin.

I am on a warpath for this. And by "this," I mean early exposure for young people to any aspect of the business or corporate world. And in the spirit of full disclosure, let me say that I am keen on seeing this happen for girls, and girls of color in particular.

Why?

Let me take a step back. It doesn't matter who we are, what we look like, where we come from, or even how young or old we are—we all want to fit in to some degree. That's just human nature. The problem is we don't all get to start off life with the same socioeconomic advantages, if any, in some cases. That's what makes the right exposure potential magic dust. I have seen how much more brightly a person's light shines with the right kind of experiences made available to them.

The rewards grow exponentially, however, when this happens in their youth. I have seen how a young girl's mind-set changes and expands when exposed to various jobs, new cultures, and world travel. I have seen how it can switch her life's trajectory from OK to OMG.

In my small hometown in rural Pennsylvania, I wasn't exposed to much that might have helped me navigate a Fortune 500 company or any corporate entity for that matter. Mind you, not that I would trade my childhood for anything. Nature was literally part of our nurturing, a privilege for which I feel supremely blessed. With the mystical Appalachian Trail as our backyard, we hiked, biked, and swam in the summers and skied and skated in the chilly winters until our cheeks were warm. As for those steaming mugs of hot chocolate Mom used to bring us by the lake after we'd finished skating, those were precious cups of liquid love.

While I went on to grow strong corporate muscles, I did so thanks to the love of adventure my parents instilled in me. I see where I used that sharpened sense of curiosity and daring to hack through my heartbreak tears and big-city fears to take aim at the Big Apple and, subsequently, the world. I see how my parents' own leap of faith—packing their bags and making a new life in Hawaii—conditioned me to see that home didn't have to be a fixed address; the world could be home anywhere. My decision to heed the call to move on came from a place inside me and from Anne's shining example of what an adventurous spirit looked like and what it could do for my life.

My success notwithstanding, I know that had I had even a modicum of exposure as a young girl to basic corporate situations, I would have found those first steps far less intimidating. I would not have seen myself as less prepared than my city-bred counterparts because I would have at least had the benefit of the corporate equivalent of a childhood vaccination. Even simple scenarios have the potential to stir whirlpools of intimidation and anxiety in an unexposed young person:

- The sight of a shiny elevator packed with people in their crisp suits and sharp briefcases

- The sound of an office with phones ringing and people talking in officious business tones

- The scent and feel of a boardroom with its imposing table and soldierlike chairs against floor-to-ceiling windows

These opportunities do not come automatically for many families.

I finally understood the implications of this not from my own experience but from my early years of mentoring women on the side. I saw more and more that while their parents had told their daughters to get a college degree and a job, they could add little else in the way of practical advice.

They could not advise their children beyond that because they themselves did not have a corporate background. They could not, therefore, suggest how one should navigate their way up and through a company. This meant that, in many ways, these women had gone into the corporate workforce blind.

The Face of Exposure

So what does exposure look like in real terms? How do you give or get this?

I'll start with the easy answer. If you own your own business and are the parent of young kids or teenagers, give them a front-row seat to your show. By exposing them at an early age, you take the edge off of the first-time jitters when it's their turn to "clock in."

- Make it a rule that they work in some entry-level capacity on their holidays.

- Let them sit in on meetings (quietly and at the side, of course) to learn what an agenda is, what a quorum is, how people interact, and how they speak in a business tone, present ideas, and answer questions posed by a superior.

- Are you in retail? Have your kids stack shelves to get a feel for merchandising. Have them interact with customers. Let them help receive goods at the back. Have them mop the floor if you have to. Show them all the moving parts that make a business work.

If you don't belong to a family that has its own business or easy access to a corporate environment, consider other options:

- Ask a family member or friend you trust about giving your child a day or two a year at their workplace.

- See if your city or community has a charity organization with a mentoring component (e.g., Big Brothers Big Sisters).

- Speak to your child's school principal to see if a partnership can be forged with a company in the community.

Inspired through Exposure

Years ago, when I was at Pfizer Inc. I met and mentored a young lady from the Dominican Republic. Sent by her mother to the United States when she was only eight, Noribel came to live with her devoted aunt, who made sure that her niece went to school every day with clean clothes and good food in her system. The only hunger she was going to let Noribel have was the good kind—the yearning for success.

As young as she was, Noribel arrived in this land of opportunity with three clear goals for which she had an insatiable appetite: to get an education, make a life, and be reunited with her mother. I don't know what that second goal looked like in her eight-year-old mind, but it was enough of a vision to propel her forward.

When as a college junior she joined INROADS, a mentoring program I had partnered with in 2000, Noribel found herself under my wing as I helped prepare her for the corporate world. Once she graduated, I hired her to work on my team at Pfizer. At that point, I took on the role of corporate mentor and chose strategic opportunities in which to give this young graduate the right kind of exposure.

I knew what a gift this was for her. I had been blessed with a similar opportunity years before when I became the newest member of the Pfizer team. My then-boss, in her attempt to help me navigate the company's culture, was careful to place me in certain beneficial positions. Not only did she set me up in meetings with key individuals, but she also ensured that I was involved in high-visibility projects.

I had had a similar experience prior to that at Xerox when I was right out of college, and then at Verizon when my new boss, Lisa Mathis—also an African American—took me upon my arrival to meet a number of folks who would be stakeholders for me. I was being heavily recruited at the time and she made sure that even my onboarding experience was seamless. This meant that for the period between my accepting the offer and walking into the company as their new employee, she kept me in raring-to-go mode, taking the time to stay in touch and send me a few Verizon tchotchkes.

When I finally walked into their offices on that first day, not only did I already feel like part of the Verizon family, but I also knew I had made the right choice. Waiting on my desk like a giant hug was a beautiful bouquet of flowers. I always aim to give my all no matter where I go. But that day I made it my mission to ensure that my boss would forever feel that hiring me was one of the best decisions of her career. I gave the company a stellar performance and a tenure that reflected my happiness.

I contrast this to my bad move experience (which I talked about in chapter 5) at another company that took the opposite strategy. I knew from day one that I was barely a footnote in their story, a feeling that was confirmed by one of my new bosses. As we sat across from each other over a meal that first week, I was advised that that would be the only "free lunch" I was going to be getting from her. Needless to say, I moved on soon after.

Once I stepped into the position of hiring, I remembered the kindness of those who had helped me settle in. When I brought Noribel to Pfizer, I paid it forward. I took her to conferences so that she could meet people. I brought her into meetings I chaired so she could see how they were conducted. I asked her questions in the presence of others so that she, and everyone else, could hear her voice (this is a strategy I use to draw out those who tend to be more quiet or introverted). And I validated her input in the presence of others.

Noribel gobbled every morsel of exposure put before her. This does not always happen. Many times we pass up on opportunities that are practically gift wrapped and placed in our hands. What was different in Noribel's case? She could have easily continued playing it small. After all, no one in her family had ever gone to college. None had held a job that required a suit and a briefcase. None had traveled or made a presentation to an audience of strangers. This beautiful, intelligent blank canvas was not aware of the many colors she could have in her world because she had never seen a fully loaded paint palette. She didn't know how big she could dream.

And yet with the right exposure, her prism changed. Why? What did she do that made the real difference? I'll tell you. She kicked fear to the curb.

I've met many such courageous young people though Sponsors for Educational Opportunities (SEO) and INROADS, organizations for college-age kids from the underserved communities of African American, Hispanic, and Eastern European descent. These are young people whose parents do not come from a corporate background. Driven by a wish to help weave these eager young minds into America's corporate fabric, the two organizations help their participants by putting them through a "corporate boot camp" and then placing them in internships with the country's Fortune 100 companies. They are resources that have seen amazing success over the years.

Once she caught a glimpse of the full spectrum of possibilities, Noribel went from taking small steps to bigger leaps. The day I witnessed her respectfully question a superior in a meeting, I knew she was growing in confidence. When at twenty-eight she embarked on entrepreneurship by buying a mini-mart in Yonkers, New York, I knew her dreams were growing, too. When she reached back and sponsored her mother to immigrate to the United States, I knew that she was in full control of her life. And when she got her MBA in 2017, I saw that her crown was firmly in place, good and proper.

More than the Eye Can See

If you're past your formative years and have already begun your career, you can still enjoy the benefits of exposure while on the job.

In chapter 3, we discussed developing a reputation for being a go-getter and team player in general by reaching beyond your immediate responsibilities. Creating exposure for yourself takes this idea a step further. It means being selective and strategic about the peripheral skills you become known for. This is what successful people are adept at doing. They keep their eyes and ears open to opportunities no matter how senior or junior their role, and they make a conscious decision to pursue them in the name of self-marketing or exposure.

You can, too.

One word of caution, however: as you make strides to elevate yourself in your career, always check your moral compass. Are you using someone solely for the purpose of self-promotion? Would you be comfortable with them doing this to you? While it's good to be strategic, it's never OK to be selfish, ruthless, or cunning. The aftertaste it leaves in your mouth can be bitter. You may get the prize, but you won't be a real winner.

Are you a millennial who can't fathom a world without constant connectivity? Good news—you're in the perfect position to become the team's resident expert in all things social media. Most companies today have internal Facebook-like collaboration tools. When such tools are implemented, younger, more social media–savvy workers have a great opportunity to showcase their skills to colleagues and bosses who may be less facile with that type of medium. Comfort with other aspects of social media—such as Twitter, Tumblr, Pinterest, Instagram—can make you *the* go-to person in your group, department, or firm. That can only happen, however, if your colleagues know that this is an area of expertise for you.

Are you a tech guru on the quiet? Do you light up when your colleagues bellyache about technology issues? "Why can't I . . . ?" "It won't let me . . . " "How do I create a . . . ?" Are you a Martha Stewart in disguise? Do you love throwing parties or get-togethers in your private life?

While some of these examples may seem like a stretch, many of these skills are useful for work situations, too. Being a natural hostess at home might mean having natural customer-relations skills or a future in public relations.

Step out of your job description. Offer solutions. Jump in. Save the day. Not only will your colleagues and superiors appreciate you more, but they'll also begin to see other facets of you. It doesn't matter what your niche expertise is:

- Using Excel
- Making use of social media
- Being creative with graphics
- Writing clear letters or reports
- Organizing small in-house events
- Giving great impromptu speeches
- Finding thoughtful and unique gifts
- Having fashion and style sense on a budget
- Using your mad grammar skills for proofreading
- Being a great hostess to newcomers or visiting colleagues

Have fun with your niche strength. Become known as the in-house guru for something to the point that people are giving your name to others as the person who can help get them unstuck. Before you know it, your name will be bandied about in offices and circles you've not yet even entered.

The Mere Exposure Effect

The mere exposure effect, simply stated, suggests that repeated exposure to something leads to a more positive feeling about it. It increases fluency, which in turn increases the positive response both internally and externally. The more often someone sees you, your skills, and insights, the more positive their perception of you will be.

So how can you turn this social psychology theory into a value proposition for your career? By taking a risk (there's that word again) and stepping onto the stage front and center. Your talent and industrious energy will be the spotlight that shines on you.

This is easier said than done, especially if you tend to be on the shy side. But each workday presents the opportunity for you to meet new colleagues, learn new skills, become an expert, and get known.

The key is recognizing these opportunities as they arise and making the most of them.

It's a Four-Way Intersection

Here's an important piece of advice to remember when it comes to seeking exposure: look for it.

While gaining visibility with your boss or your boss's boss might seem like the goal here, it is equally important to gain exposure outside of your department and with people who may have seemingly disparate or unrelated functions. In fact, you should seek exposure not just from those above you but also from coworkers and colleagues in support functions. Becoming invaluable to an administrative assistant can lead directly to exposure to more upper-level colleagues. Be useful to everyone and anyone.

Exposure: The Good

No discussion on exposure would be complete without a tip of the hat to the kind driven by social media.

The news is filled with celebrities and politicians who will do anything for public attention. Let's face it, we all have family members and friends who satisfy their craving for attention through Facebook, Twitter, and Instagram, with some even making posting a daily habit. While among the Hollywood crowd the feeling is that "any publicity is good publicity," the same cannot be said in the workplace. Yet, done tastefully in the right quantity and in the right setting, carefully crafted exposure can be a career catalyst.

Like it or not, it's a new world. We can convince ourselves that the best tactic to take at work is to keep our heads down and keep plugging along in the hopes that our efforts will get noticed. Don't get me wrong—nothing replaces solid work ethic. But no longer is this enough. In today's competitive environment, it's important to put yourself out there to get visibility and recognition for what you bring to the table. While this may not come naturally for you, you may as well embrace it and present yourself in a way that only you can.

See it as part of a day's work in your burgeoning career or business. Use exposure—the good kind—as a public relations boost. Even small doses can have a powerful compounding effect. Just be sensible about it.

Exposure: The Bad

Little needs to be said about keeping it clean when it comes to your public image. Or so you would think.

To make the point about the potential for self-sabotage through social media, I talked to my class a few semesters ago about today's job-recruiting process. With the advent of social media, I reminded them, your boss can learn much more about you than what you share in the interview.

To make the lesson real to them, I split them into groups and put them to work. The objective was to understand exactly how much a prospective employer could learn about you just from a cursory check on the Internet. Within minutes of each group beginning their research, the gasps immediately began flying up to the ceiling. Soon the overlapping chatter and the "whoa!"s and giggles filled the room.

Point made.

While I wish that more colleges—and even high schools—would talk to their students about being careful on social media, students themselves must take personal responsibility for their future. As this is the generation of reality shows, here's your reality: what you put out there *will* stay out there, like acne that won't go away. *Ever.*

Make it a personal rule to delay posting something until you've had a chance to think it over. You may be saving yourself from yourself. While an employer might allow some wiggle room for youth's lack of solid judgment, you shouldn't count on it. Sitting across the desk from you, we know only too well that you can present one side of yourself in the interview and another one on social media. So we're going to go looking because we can and want to know the real you in totality.

And don't forget that one day you might be a mother. Or an aunt. Would you be proud to let your children see your posts? Would you advise them against this kind of indiscretion? Stand out from the tired, noisy crowd. Practice prudence and restraint. Be classy. Keep it clean. Think long term.

Exposure: The Oh-So-Overdone

In 2014, Justin Bieber and Kim Kardashian topped *Forbes*'s "Most Overexposed Celebrities" list. The public had had enough of these two, fatigued of the constant photographs, media coverage, and headline grabbing. While their publicity might have added to their personal coffers, they had overstayed their welcome.

There is a fine line between exposure (i.e., visibility) and overexposure (i.e., inescapability). The bottom line here is the presence of genuine goodwill. You want to be strategic and also of real help. Good form dictates that it's prudent to be cognizant of how well your attempts to gain exposure are going. In the context of all that was discussed above, you may consider asking yourself a few questions:

- Are people seeking you out for insights, advice, or support?

- Has your self-branding as an expert in X or Y been successful?

- Do you perceive that colleagues are growing deaf to your offers to assist and see you more like a photo bomber?

- Even worse, do your efforts look more like brown nosing?

If you're in the workplace, tread lightly but confidently. Be wise enough to assess the nuances of your exposure and apply the brakes as needed.

Exposure: The Unintentional

While gaining exposure implies acting strategically, I will also be the first to admit that sometimes the opposite is just as effective, if not better. Sometimes you just wanna flow with it.

When I was working with Pfizer and in the middle of my doctorate at Columbia, a group of South Korean students came over as part of an exchange program. As my research was still in its nascent stage, I eagerly shared with the students some of my work on how to develop the particular talents and skills that individuals bring to a company's bank of personnel. I was just being me and doing what I loved. As I would soon discover, we shared the same goal: to increase the number of women in corporate roles.

In what felt like a natural next move, I invited the group to visit Pfizer so they could get a firsthand glimpse of how an American company works. More specific to our common field of research, I thought it would be a great opportunity for them to see how one works with and motivates an educated workforce, something that South Korea has in droves.

More specific to my personal experience of having once been a stranger in a foreign land, however, I wanted to pay forward the kindnesses I had received through the generosity of others. More than anything, I wanted to extend the same courtesies to these pioneering students.

I had barely finished extending the invitation when they jumped at it. I wasn't thinking of any outcome when I did this. I simply saw that I was in a position to give *them* an opportunity. Nor did I learn until after extending the invitation that they were part of an organization in Seoul that gathered speakers to present on topics in the field of human resources. When we parted, we exchanged hugs and appreciation for the generous and energetic sharing of ideas.

In 2008, about a year after the group had left, I received an invitation to be a featured speaker at the Global Human Resources Forum to be held in Seoul that year. Needless to say, my eyes went wide with excitement. I had not expected the surprise honor. I accepted the invitation immediately and made my travel plans even faster.

To this day, the Seoul invitation remains another personal reminder of why it's important to be generous of spirit and how your natural areas of enthusiasm can whisk you away on a surprise adventure.

Embrace any chance to show others a little something of yourself. Don't edit your natural curiosity. Remember, you never know who's watching.

8

HAVING POWER

("Yes, that's right. I want this.")

Some time ago I heard a story about a woman—I'll call her "Joan"—who understood the importance of power.

Then a young woman in the 1960s, Joan had just given birth to her and her husband's first child. While she had been working as a secretary prior to marrying, once she became a mother, her husband asked that she not return to work after her maternity leave and stay at home instead to raise their children while he worked to support the family. There would be more children after all, he said, and who better to look after the kids than their mother? Her reply was sweet and swift. "Yes, of course I'll do that, my darling," she said, "as long as you hand me your checkbook."

If you're in your twenties, chances are the implications of Joan's power play and the depth of her courage in standing up to her husband are lost on you. In those days, women were still in a full-on battle for even the most basic of rights. You know the story (and if not, you should make yourself familiar with it). What you may not realize, however, is that back then this social norm seeped into personal relationships and, yes, the most important of all contracts: marriage. While the love may have been equal, the power was not.

In the twenty-first century, there are still women who operate in cultures and relationships ruled by men. These women endure scenarios that may seem almost alien to some of us born and raised with more mainstream North American sensibilities. For instance, a woman's husband might discourage her from studying to improve her marketability or from working at all. He may intimate or insist that she get his permission each time she wants to use their credit card. Or he may treat her like a subordinate instead of a spouse, and even exclude her from decisions where money is concerned (such as how it's spent or invested) because she is not an income-earning partner.

Make no mistake. Control is at the center of these scenarios.

I even heard a story about a woman who was penalized by her husband for working. The couple had married straight out of high school. Always a bright and hardworking student, "Patty" was tempted by her husband's offer to treat her like a queen if she stayed at home instead of returning to the workforce once their kids were in school. She could have anything she wanted, her wealthy husband said, if she let him take care of her. She could hit the salon weekly, shop to her heart's content, and have long leisurely lunches with friends. Patty considered the offer at hand—it did sound wonderful, after all—but changed her mind within half a breath when he gave her the proviso: if she worked outside the home, she would have to support herself from her own income, no matter how small. That's when she knew that his "generosity" was a power trap.

I will leave the discussion of power in a modern-day marriage for the experts, but not before adding my two cents' worth.

Each situation is different.

What may be a beautiful symbiotic understanding for one couple may spell disaster for another, and I fully concede that cultural nuances often play a huge role here.

All I will say is this: if you're a woman married to or in a relationship with someone who won't take advantage of the fact that you're not financially independent (or not as established as they are), then by all means, feel free to explore your choices to work in the workforce or contribute from inside the home. If, however, your instincts tell you otherwise, heed them. For your own peace of mind, you might want to view a career of your own as the insurance policy you hope to never need.

One other thing.

Regardless of whether you choose to work outside of or in the home, but especially if you're in the latter scenario, sit with your partner and have them show you the lay of the land if you are not already familiar with it. Ask them to share with you the family's finances. Know where the accounts are. Get familiar with the mortgage payments and other debt-related matters. Talk about the family's income. What about insurance policies?

Have the conversation. As uncomfortable as it may feel, if your partner truly cares for you, he or she will see this as necessary and the right thing to do. I cringe when I hear of new widows lost in a blur because they don't know where their deceased spouse's bank accounts are, have none of the passwords to anything important, and are oblivious to any debt they may be in.

Oblivion is a false comfort. Find your courage. Write the questions down and read them out if you feel you need support. Use your voice. Ask. Otherwise, you're pretty much getting into a car with a total stranger without really knowing the condition of the vehicle or your destination.

The Ripple Effect of Lack of Self-Worth in the Workplace

Of all the women's issues that break my heart, self-worth gets the Grammy.

I see this struggle to be comfortable with the power within us in almost all the women I mentor and among my female colleagues in the workplace. Let me be clear: I'm referring to the use of power in a positive way, not the abuse of it. I long for the day when this becomes a nonissue.

But let's also be frank. Even though we have grown up enjoying the rights for which our predecessors so ardently fought, there are still negative connotations to the concept of women and power. Together we'll continue loosening that lid. This lack of self-worth manifests itself in our everyday lives, and particularly in the workplace. I see and hear it. Time and time again I see examples of our undervaluing the strengths we bring to the proverbial table. We think, "Oh, the skills I bring aren't all that special." "Everyone can do this." "I'm not all that talented." Or we devalue ourselves and give away our power to a superior, a mate, friends, family, or, worse, to fear.

What about the woman who holds a full-time job with crippling hours who must then go home to her second full-time job? Whether we like to admit it or not, the responsibility of taking care of the children and household still falls mainly on the shoulders of women. Yet many of us still hesitate to talk with our mates about sharing these duties. This goes even for women in top positions. Why?

This tendency to capitulate to a lack of self-worth can set in motion a crippling ripple effect. We don't simply wake up one morning and decide that today's the day we're going to abdicate our power. We do this in small ways every day, sometimes without even realizing it:

- We confuse capitulation with conciliation

- We don't speak up about something that's bothering us

- We don't ask for the terms and conditions we want in a job, partnership, or relationship (like sharing the household duties)

Before we know it, we're no longer in the driver's seat of our lives and have lost our way. If this is you, pull over to the side to stop and think. Ask yourself: Where am I really headed? And do I want to continue this way?

Crossing That Bridge

A woman I began mentoring some twenty years ago reminded me recently of how I kept pushing her to see her worth. When we first met, Yolanda was a single mother who worked as a customer service representative. It didn't take me long to see that this was a young woman who worked hard, brought genuine enthusiasm to her job, and executed her duties with the utmost professionalism.

The problem, by her own admission, was that she had grown too comfortable. Not only had she imposed limits on her abilities, intelligence, and earning potential in the workforce, but she had also accepted her situation as the end of her rainbow. For too long—and this is true of many of us—she had let society and her close nucleus of well-meaning friends suggest that she shouldn't embrace power and ambition, that she shouldn't want more than she already had. I shook my head and told her to roll up her sleeves. It was time for her to get uncomfortable.

After a couple of months of working with her (i.e., nagging her ad nauseam), I finally got her to start seeing herself through fresh eyes. Just about then, the perfect test presented itself—it was a position with a company that was located literally across the Hudson River from where she lived in Rockland County, New York. Not only was the new challenge perfect for her skill set and personality, but her commute would be a breeze. Her house was less than three miles from the Tappan Zee Bridge, the same bridge that would take her to this new adventure in Westchester.

The choice was hers. All she had to do was give full rein to her desire for true power over her life.

It was as if she were standing in front of a store, the one she always walked past on her way home each day, gazing at that shiny object on display in the window, the one she dreamed of having. She wanted it with every fiber of her being, but she couldn't picture herself actually owning it. Her feet seemed to want to move toward the door. But she was too paralyzed to walk through it.

But I wasn't going to let her just stand there.

Like my friends who literally forced me to apply to the doctorate program, I refused to let this intelligent woman squander this perfect opportunity for a leap up. It wasn't just a job—it was the potential for a brand-new life. Still battling some negative self-talk, Yolanda eventually accepted the position. She crawled across that literal and metaphorical bridge, changed companies, entered the sales field, and finally embraced her worth. Not only did she triple her income, but her self-esteem became practically infectious as her world expanded. Soon, she was practically strutting in her power. And when it came time for her son to go to college, Yolanda was able to give him the right exposure because she had finally done that for herself.

Today, she laughs when I correct her midstory. "Drag you across the bridge? *Drag* you? No, honey, I kicked your rear across it all the way!"

This only happened, however, because this phenomenal woman finally saw her true worth in all its glory. And once she got a feel for it on her skin, heard it in her voice, and felt it in her stride, it was all over. Yolanda went on to conquer even bigger challenges and build a life for herself and her son that she could not have imagined. Once she crossed that bridge, she never looked back.

How Do You Get Power?

Power, as defined by the Webster's Dictionary for Students, means "the ability or right to control people or things." But in our everyday lives, many of us might define it as the ability to influence the behavior of others. Whatever the nuances of your personal definition of power, a critical element in any discussion on this topic is identifying your source of power:

- Do you grab it however you can?

- Is it bestowed upon you?

- Are you born with it?

- Do you command it?

- Do you wait for it?

Women—especially young women—in the workplace too often wait to be anointed with power. Their perception may be that unless specific parameters of power are in their job description—that is, the power is inherent to their position—they don't have any power at all.

They couldn't be more wrong.

Quite simply, if you think you have power, you do. And if you think you don't, you don't. But here's a question: *Would you recognize true power if you saw it in all its wonderful forms?*

A Lesson from the Cradle of Civilization

Not long after I settled into my hotel room in Athens (my home for three months until I finally found an apartment), the hotel manager invited me to his son's wedding. His kindness helped me get over the shock of having actually moved to a foreign land and taught me that I needn't have felt terrified.

The Greeks, I soon learned, were a warm and engaging people. But while I arrived not knowing what to expect, I admit (with lowered head) to showing up with one preconceived notion: that women in the old world would surely be more submissive and timid than their American counterparts. Right?

The Magic of Madeleine

Ha! Was I ever wrong.

Everywhere I turned, I observed women celebrating their femininity through their attire—without apology—while at the same time shining in their signature style of power. I watched in awe. I felt as if I were witnessing an extraordinary work of art. Naturally, this phenomenon existed in the States as well, and still does, but the change in backdrop somehow made the subjects in the foreground loom even more brightly for me.

One woman in particular stood out. Madeleine was a petite, slightly plump lady in her midforties with a round face, kind eyes, pixie haircut, and gentle demeanor. Her voice, while not high-pitched, bore no tone of gravitas, either. Walking into any room, she could have easily been mistaken for being "soft."

Once she began speaking, however, you quickly understood that she was no pushover. The general manager of Greece's largest wireless company, she quietly infused that unshakable sense of self-confidence into just about every sentence she spoke, not by forcing it but by simply feeling it. The first time I saw her conduct herself in a meeting, I knew I was watching a master at work.

Her power was not just positional, it was authentic. She had been a leader in temperament all along. That, no doubt, led to her becoming one in title.

The Many Faces of Power

In her role at the time, Madeleine's main job was to pull and blend the best strengths from both companies (Greek and American) so that there'd be minimum conflict and maximum success. Madeleine was a master at building consensus. She knew how to maneuver people for the greater good.

How did she do this? Simple: by letting others feel heard.

I studied the way she comported herself in meetings. When someone else was speaking, she would give them her full attention and not allow any distractions. If someone on the sidelines started talking, she would send her hand out discreetly and gently signal for them to pause. And that was the secret to her brand of power: *she engaged in intentional listening.*

Once someone finished speaking, Madeleine would always go quiet for a moment before responding with careful thought, always including what she had just heard as part of her answer. You knew she was not just issuing a prepared response. As a result, she made her audience feel important. People came alive at her meetings. They felt energized because they had the attention of the person at the top of the food chain. What this velvet hammer got in return was even better than respect. She got commitment. And the best part about commitment is that it is self-propelling. It needs no wind behind its sails.

I would go on to find different expressions of power with the women I encountered in Jakarta and then Prague. They found ways to stand toe-to-toe with their male counterparts—yes, even behind the hijab, as was the case with my Muslim counterparts. Whether it was by applying different angles to make a point or using soft yet steady persistence to hold their stance, these women drove home the message that they were not about to dumb down their intelligence or position because of their gender, cultural nuances, or hidden faces. I watched as they executed that delicate dance between being mindful of their place in society and wielding their influence as strong businesswomen. By doing so, they influenced the outcome they wanted more often than not.

It was, to say the least, fascinating to behold.

When I finally returned to the States for good at the end of my three expat positions, I unpacked all the souvenirs I had collected. Best of all, however, was the gift I had not expected to find: a new image of power that changed me forever. It confirmed in my mind three important points:

- Women don't have to make themselves out to be minimen to have power. While we can emulate the Jack Welches of this world, we can create and celebrate our own style.

- Power is not a one-size-fits-all experience. I can be Lisa as a leader and even show my softer, nurturing side. I don't have to be loud or unyielding to assert my position.

- My signature power is my ability to combine strategic thinking while at the same time being inclusive and showing real compassion for people. And as long as I generate results, there is nothing wrong or weak about that.

There it was. I could develop my own brand of power without apology and not risk losing influence or impact. As I unpacked my bags for the last time, I exhaled and slipped into my leadership DNA as if it were a pair of cozy stilettos.

The Anatomy of Power

First things first: it is not a four-letter word. Get rid of any negative perception of power you might be harboring. I have seen talented women shy away from potentially pivotal opportunities because they associated power with being a bully or aggressor. If this is you, remember Madeleine and change your perception. Power does not have to be loud, interruptive, or pushy. Being powerful does not equal being bossy or single-minded or intractable or bureaucratic or totalitarian. It *can* mean being quiet, subtle, inspirational, graceful, and undeniably effective. Ask yourself what *your* style is. Ask how you would lead your department or company.

See power as the magic that drives progress. It can, and should, be used to influence positive change to build and create, to inspire and lift up. That's why power often shows up as benevolence. What can be more powerful than having the ability to move time, talent, treasure—and hundreds or thousands of people—for a worthy cause? Whether it's for the community's Christmas variety show or the city's animal shelter annual fund-raiser, the person (man, woman, or child) who can make it happen has the ability to wield influence.

Power is there for the taking. Seize it. Embrace it. How many times are we faced with a situation at work where we have responsibility for something but no authority? Those potential traps can be turned into opportunities to show them what you've got and claim your rightful power.

Even being a mentor to someone is a powerful position of influence.

Young women in the workplace should look for powerful women to emulate (and I'll talk more about this in the chapter on mentors). Even more importantly, all women need to think beyond the constraints of positional power and assess where their *authentic* power source may lie.

More than One Path to Power

While positional power is critical in many roles, it is not the only source of power, a point that women often fail to recognize. In 1959, social psychologists John R. P. French and Bertram Raven revealed the findings of their groundbreaking study on the bases of power, the results of which continue to be included by and large in leadership training today. As we go through each one, think of your own position in your job, volunteer position, or even home:

1. Legitimate (based on position or role)

2. Referent (based on others' loyalty)

3. Expert (based on skills or knowledge)

4. Connection (based on whom you know)

5. Reward (based on ability to confer incentives)

6. Coercive (based on ability to punish)

7. Informational (based on access to valuable facts)

Legitimate

This kind of power needs no explanation. You have the title, the role, and the nameplate on your office door. You are the one who makes decisions and leads from the front. But do you have to be in a legitimate leadership role to have power? Absolutely not.

You can also be what is known as an informal leader, someone who builds influence through emotional intelligence and courage, thereby winning the respect of others. Perhaps you're that executive assistant who's been there for years and now has deep institutional knowledge. Maybe you're the supervisor known for making smart decisions that increase your department's productivity. You could even be the young employee who shows signs of good business or people instincts. You may not sign paychecks or sit in on upper-level meetings, but when you speak others listen. And with this kind of reputation, legitimate power will eventually be yours.

Referent

Stemming from charisma, kindness or fairness, referent power comes from interpersonal skills and the way you make others *feel.*

Because you have a way of seeing their potential, colleagues willingly view you as influential because you motivate them to become better as people or team players. This makes them instinctively see you as a role model and want to pledge loyalty to you. They trust your judgment. The best part? No one can confer referent power—you take it, own it, and live it.

Expert

We've already talked about the value of becoming an expert at something. No question about it, being an expert in any area is a fast-track ticket to gaining visibility. Wherever your expertise may lie, be proud of it. And don't worry that yours may be in a narrow lane. In fact, the more esoteric, the better. (Meghan Markle—now Duchess of Sussex—used her calligraphy skills during her days as an actress to get her through her dry spells.) You always want to be a specialist, not a generalist. Once you've won market attention for being an expert in a particular area, you can always redirect that attention to other areas of your choice.

Connection

Whom do you know? Who knows you? Connection power is one of those key markers that runs the world, whether we see it or not. We're talking about access to people and to whom they know and what they know. I've learned over time that even when I hold no expertise in a particular area, I can still influence an outcome by finding and bringing aboard those who do. This releases the pressure of believing that I have to be an expert at everything. Now when I don't know the answer to a student's question, I smile and tell them, "I don't know, but I know how we can find out."

Reward

Reward and coercive power are facts of life. If you have control over the incomes or incentives of others, or have the ability to penalize them, you wield power in their eyes. All leaders need to consider how this type of power affects those on the receiving end and learn how to deploy that power wisely and fairly. And while this type of power typically rests in the hands of men, women should never shy away from holding the same reins when given the opportunity.

Informational

Informational power is a source of power that is often overlooked. On close examination, however, you can see how easily you can build this kind of power. If we buy into the stereotype that women talk more than men (we do), and tend to be better listeners and distillers of information (we are), then it means that we have access to more information than we realize. What better way to acquire power than to use an instinct that comes naturally to us? We can take what we learn and turn that into an asset by increasing our profile.

Power at Its Ugliest

No discussion today about power would be complete without addressing the elephant in the room: sexual harassment.

At the heart of the Me Too movement is the acknowledgment of power and the courage of the victims (female or male) to use their voices to reclaim it. We all know now that this particular abuse of power is another form of cowardly bullying, with the potential for even more devastating harm to the victim. It is real, it is a part of corporate America, and it is to be taken seriously.

While I sidestepped the clutches of this dark and ugly experience, I did so thanks to a few female colleagues who quickly sent me the 411. They let me—the oblivious newcomer—know whom to avoid being alone with no matter what. Still in my twenties, I was shocked that this was part of the workforce's terrain, but heeded my colleagues' counsel and took the necessary precautions.

I will forever be grateful to the women who warned me of the potential landmines ahead. And while we lament the fact that this problem still exists, we can rejoice in the changes now being made by the brave women who are speaking up.

Never forget that you hold the reins to your thoughts, intelligence, time, money, health, social life, personal life, and, above all else, your body. No job, promotion, relationship, friendship, or favor is worth a violation of any kind. Always, but always, remember that in your voice lies your power.

So do yourself a favor. Become a control freak over your own life.

9

WORKING WITH A MENTOR

("Sometimes I wish someone would just show me the way.")

I grieved for almost an entire year after my mom died.

Working at Verizon Wireless at the time as their director of talent and development, I'd come home each evening to my quiet townhouse, take a shower, pull on my pajamas, pour myself a bowl of Honey Nut Cheerios with whole milk (this was before finding out that I was lactose intolerant), and crawl into bed with the sheets pulled all the way up to my chin. I was an adult orphan now mourning the three parents I had lost. Never again would I hear their words of comfort or advice. Never again would I feel the security of knowing that there was someone in this unpredictable world who would always steer me in the right direction, even if it meant telling me that I was wrong.

But I was wrong.

Enter Toby

Six months after I finally began to notice the rising and setting of the sun once again, I picked up my life from where I had tossed it into the corner. Making good on a personal promise to further my education, I dusted off old plans to start my master's program and got the process going. At the helm of the program was its no-nonsense dean, a whirlwind of a woman by the name of Toby Berson Tetenbaum.

Toby was the kind of person you either wanted to hug hard or hide from. I say this openly because it was clear to anyone who met her even back then that the day God was handing out filters, Toby was busy with other plans. Whatever she thought, she shared—straight up. At all of five foot one, the feisty brown-haired Brooklynite walked at a good clip, spoke at an even faster one, and burned energy on the multiple roles she juggled as a university dean, lecturer, Fortune 500 business consultant, executive coach, wife, mother, and pet-dog mom. She was the kind of person you wanted to stand next to in order to catch some of that special air she was breathing.

And as if she wasn't busy enough, when our lives crossed paths that fall of 1999, she would add mentor to that list.

Shaky Start

It wasn't love at first sight, mind you. *Oh no.*

As if on a mission, Toby began challenging my less-than-sterling answers in class—much to my shock. "No," she'd muse after hearing one of my arguments. "That's not good enough. Tell me more. Explain what you mean."

I decided immediately that I was not going to like this woman.

After some time had passed, however, I realized that she was taking over where my beloved mom had left off: making me march past mediocrity and aim for excellence.

She was Anne in yet another petite, even more outspoken package, teasing out my thoughts, refusing to let me rest on my laurels, and nudging me with tough love toward self-actualization. Like my mom, Toby saw what I could become even before I could see it for myself. Unlike my mom, however, this mentor had the experience and exposure that enabled her to help me connect the dots of the corporate world.

I didn't know it then, but I needed Toby just when she appeared. And so began our informal yet exceptionally close mentor/mentee relationship.

A Challenge

One day about a year after she had become my mentor, Toby mentioned hearing about a position that had just become available at J.P. Morgan. She felt, she said, that it was tailor-made for me: vice president of talent, leadership, and executive development. Still enjoying my work with Verizon Wireless, however, I thanked her and told her that I was comfortable where I was.

"Exactly," she said with a soupçon of reprimand in her tone. "You're practically swinging in a hammock. You've already learned all you can there. And you could be doing so much more."

I didn't even attempt to argue. She was right, and I knew it.

This was not quite like the case of my friend Yolanda, whose lack of confidence blinded her from seeing her full potential. This was a little different. Toby had the benefit of experience to see that I was in cruise mode and the strength of tough love to call me out on it. It was time for me to shift to the next gear.

I let her "Lisa 2.0" vision of me sink into my own mind for all of five seconds before taking immediate action. Before I knew it, I was applying for the job that I had so quickly dismissed. I credit my faithful mentor for not only pointing me in the direction of that next major step but also with changing my life's momentum and trajectory.

I haven't seen a hammock since.

Why a Mentor?

Life can be, to say the least, challenging.

Having a mentor is very much like having a seasoned guide show you the shortcut through a maze. It's a shortcut because your mentor is advising you—usually from his or her own experience—which circuitous routes to avoid, where the potential dead ends are, and which paths have more potential to lead you to your intended destination, like becoming a CEO one day.

Sometimes a mentor is that second—and brutally honest—opinion we need. They might ask you probing, sometimes tough, questions:

- Have you thought the situation through clearly? Or are you acting hastily?

- Is there something you've not looked at? Another angle, perhaps?

- Are you making poor excuses for yourself again?

- Are you simply not trying hard enough?

- What's at the heart of all this doubt?

In my own private practice, much of my work involves helping a client see options that may not be immediately apparent. I help them see that it doesn't have to be an either-or choice—that it is possible to tweak the script and make it work for them. Or I help them see that while they're doing incredibly well, they've leaned their ladder against the wrong wall. And those, I will tell you, can be some of the hardest discussions to have.

This doesn't mean that you can't survive or even thrive without a mentor. *Of course* you can. And many have. But if you're being afforded the opportunity to forge such a relationship, why wouldn't you give yourself the advantage of benefiting from such a wonderful gift?

Naturally, you still have to take the lead when it comes to making those decisions and actually walking the path. You still do the work. You just don't need to go it alone.

And don't think there's any shame in seeking a mentor. It is not a sign of weakness—quite the opposite, in fact. Seeking guidance and learning from the wisdom of others is what smart people do. Don't believe me? The next time you meet a seriously successful person, ask them whether or not they had a mentor in their life. Chances are they'll tell you that they had several.

What Do You Need Most in a Mentor?

The short answer to this is *empathy*.

You want your mentor to have the ability to "feel your pain" and the resolve to tell you the hard truth about what you're doing or need to be doing. Think of the doctor who knows the needle will hurt yet administers the booster shot anyway because it's for your own good.

What you *don't* need in a mentor (as much as you may want it) is *sympathy*.

While it feels good to have someone commiserate with you over ice cream, showing you pity by agreeing that you have every right to feel upset is not going to get you to your goal or help you overcome your challenge. That's right. You need that tough love.

A mentor is	A mentor is not
Someone whose insights you value	The complaints department
Someone who can offer you a broader perspective	Your best girlfriend
Someone you can emulate	Your parent (unless he or she can remain firm)

Then and Now

At one time, having a mentor was a luxury or practically unheard of—especially for women seeking women mentors.

For starters, in many industries there simply wasn't a pool of senior women who might fit the bill. Second, these relationships tended to be more ad hoc and less formal. In fact, up to two decades ago, many women didn't even know that having a mentor was an option, or if they did, they didn't seek one out. The good news is that today there is no excuse. Despite the lopsided numbers—and we are all working to right that ship—there are now enough women in leadership roles to accommodate young women seeking to forge this type of relationship.

But How Do You Find One?

In my work, the most common complaint I hear from young women is that they have no idea how to go about finding a mentor. They don't know whom to ask or how to ask. Do they just walk up to someone—especially someone quite senior—and say, "Hi! Will you be my mentor?" (Ah, *no*.) Like anything else worthwhile, you need a plan.

Step One: Think

The process of finding a mentor begins long before you approach your candidate. It begins with you asking a few questions of yourself:

- What do you hope to gain from the relationship? (e.g., tips on how to avoid potential career-ending moves in week one of your first job. You want someone to help you navigate the potholes.)

- What specific skills do you hope to learn or strengthen? (e.g., do you want to be more analytical? More strategic? Better in sales?)

- What are the qualities you're looking for in a mentor? (e.g., patience? Candor?) Whatever it is, add good chemistry to your list. If you don't feel at ease with this person, it won't work.

- Is there someone whose leadership skills you admire but hope to make your own? (e.g., she is assertive, bordering on aggressive. You may not wish to go that far because you don't want everyone running when they see you, but you'd like to develop a version that's more authentic to you.)

- Are you specifically looking for someone in your industry whose expertise and experience appeal to you? You don't always have to. (e.g. I have five mentors, some of whom are not in my industry. Their emotional detachment can be helpful, as is the insight offered by those within my industry.)

- Are you looking for someone to help guide your choices as you progress in your career? Or are you looking for someone senior to provide company navigational advice to you as a new team player?

- Exactly how do you envision this person helping you set or achieve your goals?

Once you've identified the person with whom you want to work, you must be ready to tell her some basic points in order to set the tone:

- Why you've chosen her (e.g., because she's tops in sales, which is your biggest gap)

- How you hope to benefit from the relationship (refer to your answer on the previous page—e.g., avoid career-ending moves)

- What you can offer in return

Offer in return? Surprised? Yes, mentorship works both ways. And those who don't get and appreciate the quid pro quo aspect of it often find themselves in lackluster relationships. And if you think you have nothing to offer someone in a senior position, keep on reading.

Clearly defined expectations will help you both understand what your relationship is and isn't. Mismatched or unrealistic expectations on either end can quickly derail it all.

Know what you need. Look for someone who exhibits the strengths and professional or personal qualities you want to achieve. The more clear-cut your vision of what you want from this relationship, the more likely it is to succeed.

Step Two: Ask

As we discussed in chapter 4, it is well documented that women have trouble in this department. So you've done your prep work and you've got a well-thought-out plan about what you hope to learn from your mentor. You've identified the person you would like to approach. *Now what?*

- Do you call her?

- Email?

- Walk up and down the hall in front of her office and "accidentally" bump into her?

While the answer depends on what your current relationship with this person is, email is typically the most considerate way to go because it gives the recipient a chance to think about your proposal before responding. The last thing you want to do is ambush someone; it could quickly lead to resentment.

Reaching out can be scary—albeit a little less so when you know the person even just tangentially. If you're planning to approach someone you don't know, it's worth seeing if you have a contact in common who is willing to make the introduction.

Remember, you are asking a presumably busy person to make room in her schedule for you on a regular basis. In order to increase the chances of her agreeing to it, you must clearly articulate the value proposition to both parties and make it clear that you're going to be professional about this.

Ensure that your proposal clearly maps out the terms of your working relationship so that there are no surprises:

- The type of advice, guidance, or expertise you are seeking (e.g., leadership, execution, strategy)

- Frequency of meetings (e.g., monthly, quarterly) and duration (e.g., one hour or two)

- Method of contact (in person, telephone, Skype, etc.)

- What you hope to gain (e.g., develop competencies, gain industry knowledge, improve influencing skills, etc.)

- How you plan to use what you learn (e.g., improve your contribution to the team, prepare for a leadership position)

- What you hope to offer in return (e.g., a younger generation's perspectives, cutting-edge social media skills, loyalty)

Here's a sample outreach note:

Dear Ms. Johnson,

My name is Lisa Brooks-Greaux, and I am a marketing associate in the sales department.

I had the opportunity to hear you speak at the welcome lunch when I was first hired six months ago, and was intrigued by your vision for increasing market share in our industry. I am really enjoying my work at ABC Company and was wondering if you would consider becoming my mentor. Perhaps we could meet for coffee at your convenience to discuss the idea. If this is agreeable to you, we could then meet monthly or quarterly to talk about ways in which I can raise my visibility here. I'm also happy to share with you some of the innovative ideas that I have been working on with a few of my associates.

I look forward to hearing back from you.
Best regards,
Lisa

Nailing Your Role as the Mentee

"What can a senior leader possibly learn from me?"

This is a common concern that often prevents young women from going out and seeking a mentor. Think about it, though. Even though you have much less experience in your field, it may well be that your future mentor could benefit from your insight about what the experience is like for new hires at your firm, input on today's corporate culture from the younger generation's perspective, and in-depth social media or technical skills.

In today's multigenerational workforce, you might prove to be quite the asset to your mentor when it comes to gauging how well the different generations are communicating. In fact, you may even help your mentor remain relevant.

Inside the Mentor/Mentee Relationship

The successful mentor/mentee relationship is guided by a few basic commonsense rules.

Rule #1

Assume that your mentor is a busy person. Respect that and don't waste her time. Please, oh please, don't ask for information you could have easily found on your own, be it through Google or some other site. Your mentor will immediately see you as lazy.

Come to each meeting with a prepared agenda. Of course, your conversation might take you to wonderful and interesting new topics, but always plan what topic—or topics, if time allows—you would like to focus on. Be specific so that you don't waste half of your allotted hour drilling down to the real issue. Get straight to it.

Avoid vague, all-encompassing openings such as the following:

- "I want to talk to you about my career." Say instead that you've identified an area of your industry you'd like to further explore, or that you're thinking of making a switch to a related field and need some guidance on how best to accomplish that.

- "I'm having a problem in my department." Say instead that you're having a personality issue with a coworker that involves power struggle or possible sabotage.

- "I'm having a problem with my boss." Say instead that you'd like to find a way to communicate more effectively with your boss or to stand out more in his or her eyes without being obvious about it.

Rule #2

Don't complain about unfair treatment or fish for sympathy. This is still a professional relationship and should therefore remain a whine-free zone at all times.

Stay clear of the kind of weak, off-putting openers you might share with a friend or family member:

- "My boss doesn't dole out assignments fairly." Reword this. In fact, avoid the use of the word *fair*, period. Life isn't fair, and your mentor will assume that you're mature enough to understand this. Not only does it sound weak, but it also doesn't help your image. Instead, ask your mentor what you can do going forward so that you're considered for some of the choice projects.

- "I don't understand why I got such a poor annual assessment, especially when I participate more than my coworkers." As a professor, I cringe when students compare their grades to their fellow classmates' marks, particularly when it comes to participation. While I am grateful for those students who participate frequently, I am more appreciative of the ones who give me consistently thoughtful contribution. In other words, I'm looking for quality, not quantity. No doubt your boss has the same standards.

- "My life just isn't coming together. I'm not happy." Your mentor is not your parent or your therapist. She's not there to solve your personal issues. This is not your hour to vent.

Rule #3
Reciprocate. Try to bring something to the table. For example, send her a link to an article purely for her interest. Or you could send one to her before you meet that you both might like and suggest that you discuss it at her convenience.

Rule #4
Be receptive and gracious. View any kind of feedback and insight as gold. If you don't understand what your mentor is saying, ask questions and probe (*respectfully*) until you do. Be open to how others see you, both on the positive side and regarding your potential blind spots. Handling these situations with grace will be a growth experience in the comfort of what is hopefully a nurturing relationship. Work to understand the truth that your mentor is sharing with you.

Leveraging that Relationship

Let's assume that the person you reached out to agreed to become your mentor. So how do you best nurture that relationship and ensure that you are maximizing it? Your mentor can be a great sounding board when you find yourself at a crossroads or you need to make decisions that might affect your future. Remember, she is not expected to make decisions for you but rather can inform your thinking with the help of her insight and experience.

Bring specific questions to him or her:

- Should I take a lateral move that is being offered to me?

- Should I accept a transfer across the business if it's a step up?

- Should I go for that MBA? Or would I be better off getting an advanced degree of a different kind?

I don't have to tell you that mentors are often a great choice when you need a reference. Before adding them to your list, however, confirm that they're comfortable with providing a good recommendation and are OK with you giving out their contact information. The *last* thing you want is for your mentor to receive a surprise phone call about you.

Keep in mind, too, that there is an inherent shelf life in this kind of relationship. If you have lost contact with a former mentor, don't assume that you can use them as a reference three years down the road. If they're that important to you, contact them and ask first.

The Many Kinds of Mentoring

While the typical mentor tends to be someone more senior within your company, there's more choice in that box of chocolates.

Coach

One of the more nascent types of mentors is that of mentor-coach. I was fortunate enough to have had this experience with Clint Lewis, my former boss first at Pfizer and then at Zoetis Inc. when the latter broke away from its parent company to become its own entity.

Clint was, and still is, one of those bosses who could make you feel that no task or goal was beyond you. You knew when he was in the office because of the contingent of people around him, eager to glean his sage wisdom of the day, including his famous *Clintisms* such as: "More faster," "Hope is not a strategy," and my personal favorite, "What does 'good' look like?" As busy as he was in his role as the company's U.S. and international president, he always made time for others, particularly his direct reports. Born with an innate ability to zero in on people's areas of discomfort, he would challenge us to work through them and become the leaders he knew we could be. Perhaps one of my favorite examples of this came about when I had to terminate an employee. Clint knew I was uneasy about it. So he role-played the scene with me, covering every conceivable possibility until I was more comfortable. Once I delivered the news to the employee, Clint called me to see how I was doing. He showed this level care and concern to all his direct reports, without exception.

Peer-to-Peer

Not all mentors need to be several rungs above you. There's a lot to be gained by having mentors among your peers, including the opportunity to make your own trial run at mentoring, too. In a peer-to-peer exchange, you can share ideas, experiences, best practices, successes, and, of course, best goofs.

There is so much to be learned through the sharing of stories in a work environment. We become human to our coworkers and forge deeper connections that often play a big role when you're in the trenches at work or up against a tight deadline. Whom would you want in your foxhole? Would they want you? These deeper connections create circles of trust, which form the foundations for the future.

Reverse

Being mentored by a younger person is not only refreshing but it has a way of keeping you on your toes. I know this through first-hand experience.

After taking the job with J.P. Morgan, my niece Shay came to live with me in 2002. A recent college graduate some thirteen years my junior, she was working with Pfizer and loving her job. Night after night she'd come home telling me how wonderful the company was. Soon, she began suggesting that I look into a position there.

"I'm telling you, Auntie Lisa, the company's doing amazing things. It's the kind of work you'd love."

I smiled but didn't take her on. "Oh please, what do you know? You're in your twenties. *Everything's* amazing at that age!"

Of course, the joke was on me. One day, she asked me for a copy of my résumé, giving me some story about wanting to use it as a template for hers. What she did, however, was hand it over to her boss, with whom she'd been talking incessantly about my work and research. Not long after, the company contacted me for an interview. In the end, I took a position in an industry that was completely foreign to me. Thanks to my young niece, who saw something I couldn't, I took my next right step.

Stories like these, of younger women bringing along their older "sisters," abound. Oftentimes, these fresh and wide-eyed women remind us of dreams we may have forgotten, show us new perspectives, or suggest how we can adapt and thrive in an ever-changing world. Pay attention. The next time a younger woman seeks your company, asks for your opinion, makes a suggestion to you, or even pays you a compliment, what she's really doing is reminding you that you still have a lot to offer.

Mixed

We've talked about having *a* mentor, but you should really have *several* in the mix because of the different strengths they offer.

- A mentor inside your company doesn't just help with your skill gaps, she's usually the best person at helping you navigate its culture. In fact, organizations would do well to establish a bank of mentors for new employees. When I joined one company in particular, I was pulled aside by a kind executive who warned me of a certain dynamic that could potentially limit my sojourn there to only a couple of years. Thanks to her guidance, I stayed on for much longer.

- A mentor on the outside can also help you with skill gaps and help you to look at your company objectively—always useful when you can't see the forest for the trees.

- Opposite-gender mentors can give different perspective simply because of their differences in approach. We can learn a lot from them. For example, when I'm suggesting an action that takes mentees out of their comfort zone, my male mentees almost always act on it without self-editing, while my female charges (even the strongest) tend to hesitate and think on it first. That said, once they take action, female mentees tend to follow through better.

Make it your mission to get a couple of mentors on your team. *Mix it up.* The 360-degree perspective you get will help you to formulate your own goals and aspirations. *Have fun.* The more creatively you think about this process, the richer and more valuable your mentor-mentee relationship will be. And *be appreciative.* Spare time is a rare commodity these days, so your mentor's time is, without question, a special gift.

Still Watching

Today, Toby still keeps a watchful eye on me as I lead my life in my chosen direction.

While I no longer need her to push me toward self-actualization, I continue to use her amazing life as the beacon for my future. Now in her eighties, Toby, who just before press time got her real estate license, announced in early 2018 that she'll soon enter "retirement." This basically means that she'll be going into act 2 of her life, in which she'll carry only three jobs, not five. (Did I mention that she runs with her dogs when she takes them out to exercise?)

And by the way, Toby is not the only phenomenal older woman in my life who has set the bar way up there. My mother-in-law, also in her eighties, has an incredible joie de vivre that makes me want to order double of whatever drink she's having at the bar of life.

One job I won't let Toby retire from is that of mentor.

When she came into my life all those years ago, I was oblivious to the idea of needing and possibly having such a guiding influence in my life outside of my family. But even today, as a fifty-something-year-old woman, I run straight to Toby when I need someone to shake me firmly by the shoulders.

Without fail, she will serve me up some of that tough talk she usually has on tap—but always with genuine caring. I know this because now and then she'll send me an email saying that she loves me to pieces. When I take a moment to thank God for the many blessings He's sent my way, Toby is always high on that list.

So what are you waiting for? Go out there and find your Toby.

10

LEANING ON YOUR PERSONAL VILLAGE

("I need a team that never takes vacations.")

The following is a standard version of an almost weekly (and by weekly, I mean monthly) telephone conversation between my brother, Joey, and me—unless I can't reach him, in which case I call my friend Michele and have a slightly different conversation but with the same result. (And please don't ask me whether I named my brother after our dog or vice versa because I was still a kid then and honestly can't remember.)

"Skippy!"

"Leesee! What's going on, girl?"

"The usual! This 'n' that. Busy, busy, busy!"

"Well, that's you."

"Yep! So how's the weather in Orlando today?"

"Not a nor'easter in sight."

"That's why you moved there!"

"Lisa?"

"Uh-huh?"

"You're at the gym, right?"

"Yep!"

"Stalling again, right?"

"Yep!"

"Parking lot?"

"Like the last time! And the time before that!"

"In the car?"

"Uh-huh!"

"Get your butt in that gym. This is me hanging up now. Goodbye."

(click)

Not a Game of Solitaire

In the world of navigating the workforce, the mantra has long been *networking, networking, networking.* And it's true—the more people you're connected with, the more contacts you have to reach out to when looking for a new job or career, and, by extension, the more opportunities you have available to pursue.

Networking sites like Facebook and LinkedIn make connecting with former classmates and colleagues easy. How truly mind-blowing it is (for those of us who grew up without such tools) that LinkedIn and the like can transport us back to our grade-eight classrooms and put us in touch with classmates we have not seen or spoken with in forty years. Then imagine finding out that the weird artsy kid who used to sit behind you in second period now owns that hot furniture design company you want to work for.

But while being able to cast a wide net is an advantage, having a rock-solid inner circle of support is paramount. A personal village is a group of people in your life who, separately or together, form your cheering section. They are your tireless, faithful champions who encourage and challenge you to be your best self. And because these individuals genuinely care about you, competition never comes into play. With this motley crew, you never have to look over your shoulder.

Your Personal Decoding Department

Your village does so much more than encourage you from the side-lines, however. They roll up their sleeves and get to work with you even if it means getting a little muddy. These trusted individuals are the advocates who act as our sounding boards, advisory committee, or life-size mirrors that show us ourselves when we are confronting a difficult choice, challenge, or change.

They are effective at this because they know us. They've figured out our algorithm. Oftentimes, they see something in us that we overlook in ourselves. Their insight helps us open up to possibilities that we may not have otherwise had the courage to consider.

They might be our closest friends, mentors, or sponsors. And with each bringing to our life different strengths and personalities, some may fill more than one of these roles.

Like a doctor with her prescription pad in hand, this posse is often adept at diagnosing what ails us and prescribing corrective steps. They might prod us to take more risks or try something new. Maybe take a simpler route. Sometimes they point out the uncertainties of a situation we're in and help us to consider a more tempered approach. And sometimes, especially if they were a witness to our youth, they remind us of just how much we've grown.

Take a moment to ask yourself who your sounding board is. Why do you turn to them as opposed to someone else? And how specifically have they helped you?

Clutch or Shoulder Bag?

Consider this: when you're getting ready for a date, don't you sometimes ask friends for their opinion on your outfit? "Should I wear the red shoes or the black?" "Hair up or down?" "The clutch or the shoulder bag?"

You ask not because you're incapable of making a decision but because you value their point of view and insights, and because, yes, sometimes you just need input that you hadn't considered. They may tell you that you look great in orange-red but not cherry red. And they may point out that if you wear the shoulder bag, your hands will be free to hold your plate as you enjoy the appetizers. No question about it, you're capable of getting dressed for an event or date without a committee. But isn't it more fun this way?

Imagine, then, the value this posse can add to your life when you're faced with serious life-shaping decisions.

Does It Really Take a Village?

While many people associate the phrase "It takes a village to raise a child" with Hillary Clinton, it is actually an old African proverb. The spirit behind the quote suggests that it takes the care and influence of many—men and women, old and young—to create the most nurturing and positive environment for a child to grow and succeed in. This idea has a profound meaning for women and men at all ages and stages of their lives and careers. The bottom line?

We're always going to be people who need people.

When I was halfway through writing my doctoral thesis, I got to a point where I was the human equivalent of stale gum on a hot sidewalk—I was beyond stuck. Juggling my energy between my position at J.P. Morgan, my mentoring work, and my life at home, I was one all-nighter away from collapsing. Unable to contain my frustration, I went from open sighs to outright wailing about wanting to throw in the towel. "Whatever! I'm done!" I'd say when at my worst. "I don't care anymore about the stupid doctorate!"

One Friday evening, my friend Denise arrived at my doorstep with a determined look on her face. "You're going to graduate," she said as she barreled past me, plopped down her handbag, and pulled off her olive-green car coat. "Giving up is not an option."

She had gotten her doctorate the year before and was going to see to it that I finished mine. Setting up camp in my kitchen with flip charts on every available surface, she instructed Carl to supply her with hot tea and warm socks. Once our temporary bunker was ready, we shut out the world and got down to work. And when it became clear that she was going to be staying overnight, she asked Carl to get her a toothbrush.

Denise did this with me, *for* me, for the next seven weekends in a row. To say that she gave up her free time doesn't begin to describe the time and energy she sacrificed for my benefit. As her dear mother had passed away not long before this, Denise was also in need of some shoring up herself. And yet here she was—this generous woman, loyal friend, and embodiment of courage—walking over the coals with me just so I could get to the other side, too.

You Don't Scare 'Em

This was not the first time Denise was there to rescue me. She was one of the two J.P. Morgan colleagues who had convinced me to apply for my doctorate to begin with. The second half of that team was another brilliant friend by the name of Pierre. More on Pierre in a bit.

Like my brother, Denise and Pierre knew me well enough to choose the most effective strategy: don't give Lisa a chance to speak or change her mind. In the "Facing Failure" chapter, I mentioned that they even mailed in my doctorate application for fear that I'd choke.

What I did not tell you, however, is that these two had actually hauled me into the conference room at the office, locked the door, and held me hostage as I filled out said application. They knew exactly which guerilla tactics to employ in order to save me from myself. And being free to be your flaw-filled self in your imperfect world—without fear of judgment—is like slipping into a hot bubble bath at the end of a long day.

Our personal village is many things to us:

- *The drill sergeant we need when struggling to maintain our standards.* When I make that call to my brother, Joe, from the gym's parking lot, I do so knowing that he's going to do his job and jettison that bad angel off my shoulder—the one telling me that I can skip the gym because I went once the week before. No matter how many times I try to use him as a stalling tactic, he'll shame me into that gym.

- *The harbor we take refuge in when being swallowed by a storm.* When I need to have a good moping session (and even the toughest among us do now and then),

I call Michele. I know she will have soothing words, a warm hug, and lifesaving treats on hand to get me through those turbulent waters. And yet, even she will tell me when it's time to quit crying and head back out to sea. In our village, we don't let each other wallow for long. That kind of cop-out behavior is for other people.

- *The cheering team that pops up when you least expect it.* Even right before a business meeting, they'll hold hands in a circle in your office, bow their heads, and ask God to make your boyfriend, Carl, pop the dang question already this weekend since he missed your birthday *and* Valentine's Day.

- *The friendly jeering team that keeps you honest.* They'll burst out laughing when they find out that you, a big-shot PhD graduate, failed a certification course like a swan-dive-turned-belly-flop because you tried to wing it instead of studying the material to death as you usually do. And then they'll give you that look—the one that tells you that they expect you'll have better news to report the next time they see you.

Hall Monitor

Ideally, the best candidate for your circle has a touch of hall-monitor monster in them; he or she is loath to issue passes and entertain your sorry excuses. If you have one among them who is steel-trap strong, make that person your goals-accountability partner, as I did.

At the start of each year, Michele and I exchange goals lists, and then we check in with each other monthly. We always get straight to the point:

- "Where are you with this?"

- "Do you need some help with that?"

- "Hey, that due date has come and gone. Why?"

- "That's not your best work. Can you improve on it?"

- "You seem stuck. How can we get you to the next step?"

It is a dream partnership I could not do without. It means knowing that while I'm responsible for doing the work, I am not alone on this journey. Young professional women, especially, should look to create and foster these bonds. These boot-camp friends make us all better. And because we know what each other's goals are, we keep an eye and ear out for contacts, information, and opportunities that may come our way and hand them over.

Mastermind Groups

Another avenue to consider taking is a mastermind group.

Those of us who have tried them (yours truly included) swear by their effectiveness. Mastermind group members are self-motivated professionals and entrepreneurs from various unrelated industries and walks of life whose common denominator is the hunger to do something amazing with their lives. These synergy-fueled groups meet once or twice a month to suggest concrete steps you could take to achieve whatever goal it is you want to conquer.

Say you want to start a business. Take your start-up to the next level. Move up the ladder in your department. Market your book online. Launch a new product. While you'll receive words of encouragement from this group, the primary goal here is progress. You will leave with concrete actionable suggestions in your notepad (or laptop if paper is foreign to you). These groups speak specifics. I have been meeting with mastermind groups for some eighteen years now. It's like having your personal ATM of ideas. Find the right mastermind group for you by searching online, asking friends, or looking at Meetup.com. And if that doesn't work, you can always start your own.

My Personal Village

You know the saying "Show me your friends, and I'll show you who you are." If this is true, then I must be a pretty fabulous person.

Allow me to introduce you to my village. Collectively, these special people reflect my core values. I respect their insights and perspectives, even though they may sometimes differ from mine. I have gathered these individuals along the way from my workplace, classroom, and social circle, and I hold them in the highest esteem. Each plays a unique role in helping me stay the course in the marathon of life. For them I would run out of my house and into my car in my pajamas if I ever got that emergency call at three in the morning.

As I describe my relationship with each one below, think about your own circle of friends. You may recognize qualities in them that you never saw before:

Bridgitt. Bridgitt is a former work colleague who became my close friend. A strong strategic thinker, she is someone I count on when I want to think through a complex issue with lots of disparate moving parts. She just has that innate ability to stand back and look at the situation with fresh eyes. Bridgitt is also a natural and gifted connector who is generous in making introductions within her vast network of colleagues and friends. When I need to know where to find something, or someone, Bridgitt is my go-to Google girl. I have yet to hear her say, "I don't know."

Denise. By now you know all about Denise. I met this super fireball while we were at J.P. Morgan. At the time she was at Columbia studying for her doctorate degree. Blown away by her indomitable spirit, I watched this amazing woman blaze a path toward her goals regardless of whatever meteor shower was heading her way. I know that in her I have someone who will never let my weary knees touch the ground.

Michele. This is my happy friend who is always pointing out the good in the world. Michele's fountain of optimism constantly nourishes and inspires me with just the right amount of realism. This kind soul has not a judgmental bone in her body, and will first search for the positive in any person. I turn to her when I want to take a more compassionate approach to working through a situation that is particularly thorny or when I just need to hear that everything is going to be OK.

Pierre. Also a former colleague, Pierre is my rock-star strategist and one of the smartest people I know. American-born of Jamaican descent, Pierre exudes that quintessential Caribbean-cool swagger, almost to the point of appearing nonchalant. This, of course, makes him my polar opposite.

Pierre never asks the obvious. He'll be the one to flip a narrative on its head and view it differently, a technique that helps hone my own strategic muscles. My friend never fails to give me counsel that goes straight to the heart of whatever conundrum I'm facing. And taking it straight to the core *is* his specialty. "You, Lisa, always bite off more than you can chew," he once observed quietly, "but then you keep on chewing until it's all gone. You always figure it out."

Pierre first shared this insight with me some twenty-five years ago. Since then, I have reached for it like a vitamin supplement whenever I feel overwhelmed or panicked by a mammoth project. And when I left that "failed" job within months of taking up my position, he not only pointed out that it took courage to leave, but he also reminded me that I would be saying the same thing to a client who had found him or herself in the same position. And he was right.

Toby. What more can I say about Toby? I first met her in the classroom, where she consistently challenged me despite my attempts to hide in the shadows. That sparring forced clarity into my own thinking, a strength that has since become a hallmark of my approach to solving any new puzzle. Now that *I'm* standing at the head of the classroom, I push my own students the way she pushed me. I don't hesitate to say that I have grown before Toby's eyes, and that we have grown to respect each other enormously.

Each of these individuals is extremely dear to me for the friendship, counsel, support, and guidance he or she provides. And while they are my go-to resources when I am facing a challenge, I also nurture these relationships when all is going right in my world. We hug and squeal (Pierre doesn't squeal, of course) and jump up together in a happy dance (Pierre's not doing that either) no matter who's sharing the good news. They also know they can't leave me, ever. If they did, I would pretty much hunt them down and drag them back home.

A Word on Parents

When I was seven, I got into trouble at school for talking when I shouldn't have.

My punishment, as issued by my teacher, was to sit in the boiler room the next day for lunch. This was all explained in the note she gave me to be signed by my parents that evening. The next morning, while having breakfast, I handed my father the note for his signature, thinking that that would be the end of it.

"Oh? So you were talking in class, were you?" he said with surprise, the note still in his hand.

I replied in between mouthfuls of oatmeal with a casual "Oh yes, and I'm sorry, blah, blah, blah." But then he began biting on his lip. It was a sign I knew well. It meant that my dad was not happy.

"And for *this* you're expected to eat your lunch in the *boiler* room? With the *male janitor* there? *Alone*? I don't think so. Get your things. Let's go."

The next thing I knew, my father was escorting me to school that morning with the note still unsigned. He explained to the teacher and principal that while he agreed that I needed to be reprimanded for my "crime," he did not agree with the punishment.

"There's no question that our daughter misbehaved. And her mother and I will deal with her," he said as I stood there, mortified at the conversation taking place a couple of feet above my head. "But this is no way to treat a child. No daughter of mine is going to be sitting in any boiler room where there is the potential for an explosion."

With that intervention, my punishment changed from lunch in the boiler room to two weeks of evenings in my room at home without talking. I was not allowed to utter a word. There would be no phone calls, no playing, nothing. After two days, I was practically traumatized. But after two weeks (my parents stuck to their promise), I had learned two things: One, disrupting the class gets you in big trouble. Two, having caring parents gives you an edge.

You may wonder, therefore, why in the chapter on mentoring I advised against putting your parents in the category of mentor. I don't mean to suggest that they are not qualified to help guide you but rather that the role they play is different. I still think that, to a large extent, it takes a special kind of parent to achieve a sense of detached compassion. Here, I am describing parents who can honestly and *consistently* separate their role as the one who gave you life from their role as the one who gives it to you straight when it really counts. Such are the complicated dynamics between parents and children that, far too often, the lines get crossed. And understandably so. As children, we, too, blur our own messages by testing our parents in ways that we would not test others.

As it turned out, I took the lessons and confidence my parents instilled in me to turn within and think through my own problems or situations.

It wasn't an attempt to hide from them or to shut them out. Rather, it was an exercise in trying out the wings they were helping me to grow. Once I had decided on a course of action, I always brought my parents into the fold. For this reason, they will always hold an honorary place in my personal village.

And even though I no longer have them here, I will always have the memories of those moments when they held firm for the sake of my secure future.

Pick, Choose, and, Yes, Sometimes Refuse

In chapter 1, we talked briefly about the relationships (of the platonic kind) that you should be seeking to add to your life. And while it's only natural that our friends all bring different life experiences to the table, they should all have one common denominator: the wish to see you grow and thrive. Unfortunately, this is not always the case.

When you detect detractors in your midst, by all means give them a chance to change. No one is perfect. Everyone has an off day. But if they continue to disappoint, if you see a toxic pattern developing, consider confronting them or moving on, for your sake. Do not view this as a loss. If they truly value you, they will come around. And if the terms are right, you'll be ready to welcome them back with outstretched arms.

I know from personal experience how difficult and painful this can be. While I have only had to do this once in my life, the memory of it alone still makes me wince to this day.

"Jackie" became a friend of mine following my college years. A lovely individual with a good sense of humor and great plans for her life, she took me under her wing and showered me with her protective big-sister side. For years I relaxed in our friendship as if it were a warm blanket fresh from the dryer. Even our families became friendly with one another.

After a while, however, I began to notice an uncomfortable pattern. Each time I met up with her, my joy balloon full and taut as it usually was, I would inevitably leave her company feeling mildly deflated. While I was still floating, I was now more like a soft balloon. This feeling was so insidious that, at first, I completely missed it.

One day, after feeling that nagging "huh" in my bones a little more than usual, I decided to put our friendship under a microscope. It took objective observation on my part, but I eventually realized that while my friend would *say* positive things, her tone and body language would quietly counter it. It was, in fact, negativity disguised as humor. And this usually happened, I realized with heavy sadness, when good things were happening for me.

When I finally saw the whole truth, I was devastated. She was a good person, and we had spent many years investing in our friendship. I probably would have tolerated this new revelation for the sake of our long history. But when I saw that I was getting into the habit of tamping down my exuberance just to make her more comfortable, and fast becoming the kind of person who saw her glass as half empty, I had to reexamine our friendship. The person I was becoming around her was not someone I recognized.

Fleeting moments notwithstanding, I had always been a generally positive person. That's just how my DNA was wired. So when I realized that time spent with this friend was costing me my natural-born upbeat outlook, I knew I had to walk away.

Setting Your Standards

I share this story to make the point—again—that choosing friends (your village members) is not to be taken lightly. And I'm not talking about the occasional good-time friends you see now and then at happy hour. Those casual—even superficial—relationships have their place and purpose in your life. And as long as you understand this and keep your expectations of them in check (translation: don't overinvest and don't expect great dividends), you should find some pleasure in those, too.

Instead, I'm referring to the people we let into our personal space habitually. In many ways, it's like deciding on the kinds of food you're going to put into your body every day. Is it going to be junk or healthy food? Take a serious look at your choice of friends.

Ask yourself:

- Is the friendship weakening or strengthening you?

- Later on in life, will you be paying the price or reaping the benefits of this long-term exposure?

- Are they investing in you as much as you are in them?

- Do they seem to want the best for you? Do they cheer you on and ask about your progress? Or do you sense them pulling away when you're getting somewhere?

- Do you learn important life lessons from them? Or are they great examples of what *not* to do?

- Are they challenging you to get your act together, or are they giving your not-so-healthy habits a pass?

- Do they seem comfortable in mediocrity?

- Or, worse, are they secretly projecting their issues on you as their way of acclimating to their own struggles?

In other words, are they, whether intentionally or not, trying to dethrone you? Remember, no one is perfect. We are all hopelessly flawed. Like anyone else, we'll have our off days, too. But if ever you're in doubt of your place in a friend's heart, always remember the litmus test of a healthy relationship: just as a real friend won't let you drive drunk, a real friend won't let you get away with murdering your own potential.

11

REINVENTING YOURSELF

("Will I be able to handle what life throws at me?")

My childhood backyard was filled with apple trees. Each autumn, my brother and I would go walking among them to check on our awaiting bounty. When Joey saw one that was laden with fruit, he'd climb up, tell me where to stand, and then shake the tree with a fierce grip so that the apples would rain down on my head. He'd always laugh while I pretended to protest.

Our family life was this portrait of idyll. From skating on glistening frozen lakes to exploring lush mountain trails to eating home-cooked dinners together at our table while talking about our day, we lived what most only saw in movies. But when our father got sick and died, our world as we knew it was shattered. And so we put our trust in God and did the only thing we could: reinvent ourselves.

Often Born Out of Necessity

Admittedly, challenging circumstances are usually the spawning ground of reinvention. When we lost our beloved father, the family's main breadwinner, we closed rank and became the three musketeers. We did what we had to do to survive as a family.

Mom took that better-paying job at the factory and leaned on neighbors more to help watch over her children. Joey and I focused on our schoolwork and sports, ensuring that Mom never had to worry about our grades or conduct. The last thing she needed or had time for was a meeting with a teacher or the school principal.

On Friday nights, we'd dine at Matteo Dave's Pizzeria and share a large pizza with sausage and pepperoni on one side and cheese on the other. If Joey had an away game for basketball or football, we'd have our pizza dinner and then literally drive behind the school bus to the game. We did this out of necessity. Mom was not the best at directions, and GPS was still a dream in someone's wild imagination. After we got back, we'd get ice cream at the nearby Dairy Queen. I'd always stick to my favorite, vanilla dipped in chocolate. And if there was no away game, Mom would take us to the neighborhood YMCA so that we kids could swim. Not yet a swimmer at that point, Mom would watch us from the side, ready with our dry towels once we'd had our fill. That was our new life and the new family nucleus we became, at least until my stepfather became a part of our lives.

While I will always regret the loss of my biological father, the painful experience of learning how to adjust and reinvent myself, jolting as it was, was one that would help prepare me for life and all its unexpected twists and turns. Looking back, I know exactly when I saw this skill in play.

I witnessed it in my mom, not only when she picked up the pieces after our loss but also when she eventually remarried and moved to Hawaii with my stepfather. This, in turn, forced me to adjust to the fact that I had lost my familiar touchstone. I engaged my reinvention skills when I took that first overseas position in Greece to get over a personal hurdle. I employed them yet again in Indonesia, a country that looked, felt, and smelled like nothing I had ever experienced, with its jarring heat, exotic spices wafting into the air, pedestrian and vehicular traffic that included goats, and a language that was as close to English as steak is to quinoa. "Now you've really done it, Lisa," I said to myself in a panic on my way in from the airport. But still, I thrived.

I reinvented myself again when I became a wife, pursued my doctorate, and changed industries midcareer. And when I left that job that did not move to the rhythm of my soul only to successfully reignite a long-standing goal I had placed on the back burner? Yep, I did it again.

Change—It's the Way of Life

There are many times in our lives when we find ourselves facing the prospect of shedding old skin for new. Sometimes it feels like a good option ("I *want* to"). At other times it might feel like the only option

("I *have* to"). No matter the catalyst, the process of self-reinvention involves self-discovery, self-awareness, courage, and a fundamental openness to change.

Remember going from elementary school to middle school? That's a time when kids often choose to change their image and become a new person in a new school. Sometimes they do this by transforming their bodies, changing their style of dress, or taking up a sport when they've never been the athletic kind.

Some will take on a persona at summer camp that's different than the one they have at home. And others may choose to become Barbara at college instead of Barb. But reinventing ourselves is a dynamic process that can, and should, be applied at various stages of our lives, even as adults. After all, it's only natural.

And in many cases, it can do us a world of good.

We Do It

So why would adults want, or need, to reinvent themselves? The reasons vary from the simple to the significant:

- You've lost interest in a chosen career and decide to transition to a new field.

- You've overcome an illness or other serious setback that changed your life's trajectory.

- You took a break from your career to look after children or elderly parents and can now focus on you again.

- You now have two or more children to put through college—maybe even at the same time.

- The soft economy has thwarted your plans, forcing you to tweak and adjust.

- Your personal situation has changed (e.g., marriage ends, spouse becomes ill or has life-changing accident), requiring you to become self-sufficient or even the family's breadwinner.

- You've left your homeland and are now making a new life in a new country.

If you're fresh out of college and starting out, you may not see yourself in these next few pages. I encourage you to read on nevertheless. This may be you one day. Or it may be someone close to you—even your mom. Regardless, it'll be good for you to take a peek at your options down the road should you ever feel you're caught in a challenging position or have become restless for something more.

Confessions of a Transformation Artist

In 2010, I was caught in the middle of what can only be described as a perfect storm.

Then the director of executive development at Pfizer Inc. I was pursuing my doctorate while joining the nationwide struggle of surviving an economy that had gone *Titanic* on us. As if life hadn't become complicated enough, the pharmaceutical industry was going through a difficult transformation of its own. Over in our corner, the company downsized my department to a team of one—me. My daily round-trip commute, which sometimes reached anywhere from two and a half to three hours daily, robbed me of the little personal time I had to exercise and unwind. And, to top it off, I couldn't help but secretly feel that gone was the wiggle room I might have previously had for unforced errors.

Drowning in stress, I began self-soothing with food—and not always the good-for-you kind. Before I was ready to admit it, the scale was telling me that I was fast approaching the two-hundred-pound threshold. "Your sugar and blood pressure levels are way up there," my doctor said one day during my annual checkup. "A first for you, Lisa. What's going on?" She was concerned. So was I. But I did nothing about it.

One night, sleep became a date that had stood me up. For weeks I tried to hack my way into getting even five measly hours of slumber so I could recharge. No luck. I would force myself out of bed each morning, my eyes burning with fatigue, my spirit already heavy as I trudged into the bathroom to get ready for another day. One morning, the skirt I was pulling on stopped midway up my hips. So I did what I should not have done—I began buying new clothes a size up. I did this a couple of months later for a second time. Then a third.

Finally, I returned to my doctor. For one month she had me avoid all refined sugars, reduce my meal portions, and increase my intake of water (half my weight over the period of a month, to be exact). By the end of the month, I had lost ten pounds and stopped living unconsciously. I'd become mindful again. By making the turnaround in my health, I had begun the process of returning my appearance and outlook to one I recognized and liked.

Back in control of my health, I went on to lose forty pounds in all. I even began wearing the color red once again—high heels included—simply because I knew it made me look my best. It made me feel like holding my chin up that much more. And, like it or not (and I do wish sometimes we didn't have to pay attention to the superficial), how we feel when we look at ourselves matters. Regardless of your gender, that's just how we are.

Companies Do It

Admittedly, the term *reinventing* may seem hyperbolic. But if you think about it, we are constantly tweaking ourselves even when we think we're simply moving on to the next "natural" stage of life: marriage, further education, new jobs or careers. We need to be adaptable enough to zig and zag and go with the flow.

This is, of course, easier said than done. And yet, even corporate giants who have the power to give the stock market a cold with a single sneeze eventually have to take a turn on the dance floor with reinvention.

In my other life as a corporate executive, I saw where my then-employer—a long-standing and respected Fortune 500 giant in the automotive industry—had the good sense to pause and rethink how they did business. In the past, as was the case with just about any other entity that produced a consumer item or service, this company had long enjoyed the luxury of focusing mainly on its product, target consumers, and industry competitors.

What they did not see at first, however, was that another seemingly unrelated force was now impacting just about everything they did. And its name was *data*. This meant the company had to change its approach to marketing and pay attention to what Google, Amazon, Facebook, and other data-gathering entities were doing.

My former employer was not alone.

In this wild new frontier, a car manufacturer's main concern is no longer another maker of automobiles. A pharmaceutical company's biggest hurdle is not another drug company's newest painkiller. You get the picture. But if this super giant had not stopped to adjust its focus and reinvent its approach in general, it would likely be gone from the picture today.

Even Countries Do It

And what about entire nations of people? Even they walk away from the past in the name of making themselves anew. Ironically, it was while I was in the process of reshaping my own life that I saw such an example.

While in Prague, my third expat position in a row, I witnessed the formerly communist Czechoslovakia transition to what is now the Czech Republic. Still in its nascent stages of settling into a consumer-driven economy, I saw teething pains even in the minutiae of everyday living.

Store clerks, unaccustomed to having to charm the cash out of customers' pockets, were now straining themselves to offer something they themselves had never known before: customer service.

The Czech people in general, previously accustomed to being told by their leaders what to think, do, and accept, were now wading cautiously into the open sea of self-reliance and free thinking. While the discomfort was palpable at times, the country's citizens nevertheless led the revolution to reinvent their lives. They pecked away at the government until it fell. By taking back their country, they took back their power and their future.

Sign of Failure or Success?

We often associate reinvention with something negative—a failure of sorts resulting in having to switch to a plan B. And, sure, sometimes it is.

But that hardly puts us in the minority. Even the most successful among us have had to turn to reinvention as a result of plans gone rogue. I'm not suggesting that we flee an unhappy situation in a knee-jerk reaction (which is what reinvention would be without the benefit of introspection). Instead, we should be like the success-minded individual who sees reinvention as part of personal growth and development.

The catalyst can also be a positive, even proactive one. Maybe your passions have shifted. Maybe you simply have an instinct that a change is needed. The point is that reinvention, done in the spirit of a positive makeover, can give your life a much-needed boost.

Take complacency, for example. In my own career, as I shared in the chapter on mentoring, I had grown exceedingly comfortable in a job at which I excelled. Without realizing it, I was holding that double-edged sword. Moving along with a steady wind in my sails, I was failing to notice the signs of more-challenging opportunities slipping past me. And while that was by no means a tragedy, it was, at the very least, a huge what-if in the making.

Ironically, I went on to become a master at seeing where, and how, human resources reinvention was needed in the corporate setting, eventually becoming known as a "quiet disrupter." But soon after realizing that this was not a one-size-fits-all experience, I changed how I pitched change to others. Now, instead of pushing them along, I bring them along.

The Mothers of Reinvention

Even though I have never been a mother, I respect these patient molders of young minds the most. While having a job or career is truly something to be proud of, you're usually only hurting yourself if you make a mistake. But raising another human being? I have watched with wonder as friends carry out this crucial role of shaping the next generation. I'm with Oprah here. That's the hardest job in the world. Period.

And yet it's no secret that mothers who work outside of the home are still made to defend their ability to balance their careers with their at-home duties, an ability that men are rarely, if ever, questioned about. It is a dialogue we must change. In time, and with the right nudging of corporate America for more support in this area, we will. Zoetis, I should proudly add, is one such company. When it became an independent company in 2013, its management focused on making the organization a place where women could advance their careers while raising their families. As executive sponsor of its women's council, I worked ardently with the team to do just that. The very next year, in 2014, Zoetis was recognized by *Working Mother* magazine as a top ten company to work for, an honor it continues to receive to this day.

But what of the woman who cut short her career for her family? What of the woman who sacrificed a working life altogether so she could keep the home fires burning? These women are, in my humble opinion, perhaps the most vulnerable among us.

In recent years, this large cohort of stay-at-home mothers has received a lot of attention. In most cases, these are well-educated women who are returning to the workforce after a career break. Oftentimes, these breaks lasted several years—ten or more in many cases—rendering their skill sets stale or, worse, obsolete. Reinventing yourself in these circumstances can be enough to make you feel as if you're about to cross the street in the path of oncoming traffic.

Stop and think about this woman's position for a minute. Can you feel her heart racing as she prepares to face a workforce that's younger, fresher, and more current? Can you picture her sitting in an interview, wondering how she's going to convince the person sitting behind the desk to hire her when she's been driving carpool for the last decade? While each returning-to-the-workforce mom comes with her own set of concerns, there is one that they almost all share: "Do I have enough to offer?" or, even more heartbreaking, "Do I have *anything* to offer?"

I have had the privilege of speaking with some of the brave women championing this group. Their stories remind me that life can throw you curveballs that send your world in directions you never imagined. While I concede to them that I fully appreciate their fears, I also tell them that they need to look at them differently. I tell them that, not for nothing, but if they've spent the last ten or more years getting the kids to school five days each week, shuttling them to extracurricular activities almost as often, attending PTA meetings where tensions can be high, fund-raising with the school or other groups, sorting out squabbles, caring for a child or elderly parent with serious health challenges, tending to meals and laundry day in and out, and even looking after a pet or two, then *yes, they have skills that are transferable.*

This is where the exercise of taking stock, which we'll address in the next chapter, becomes your secret weapon. Dig deep. Be objective. Talk to yourself as if you were counseling your best friend. While the package is different and certain technical skills are missing, you know only too well that a work-in-the-home mom is experienced in several areas:

- Budgeting and planning
- Conflict resolution

- Decision-making
- Motivating others
- Seeing through the smoke
- Time management
- Teamwork

I also tell these ladies that they need to change their language. Emotions are infectious. People sense your mood from your body language alone. The words that come out of our mouths only serve to confirm what you're already emitting. Smile and you'll seem approachable. Scowl and you'll be the last person people want to talk to. You get the idea. The same goes for our confidence. So when these women come to me and begin our conversation by qualifying their situation with "I'm only a stay-at-home mom," I stop them midsentence. I make them change that. I point out that they have to prime the interview in their favor. And I tell them to try this for an opener instead:

"I have been a stay-at-home mom for XX years. Let me tell you what I've learned and how I've performed in that role. Let's talk about how I mastered budgeting, goal setting, and motivation. Let me tell you how we moved as a family several times because of my husband's job and how I made our relocations seamless for our family. Let me tell you how I homeschooled my son so that he could earn his high school diploma while battling a debilitating condition that made attending traditional school impossible. Let me tell you how I helped my daughter navigate the current social stressors of bullying that affect today's teens. Let me tell you about how tech-savvy I had to get just to keep up with them. Let me tell you about the birthday parties I organized year after year. Let me tell you about the role I played in the PTA and the goals we accomplished under my leadership. Let me tell you about the money we raised through numerous events that required detailed planning and careful execution, all while I had to diplomatically navigate the many parents involved and their management styles. Let me tell you how I ran my household like clockwork. Let me tell you how I ensured that our bills were paid on time and our pet dog never missed his heartworm pills. Let me tell you how I became head of research when the time came for my kids to apply to college. Let me tell you how I helped my husband with his startup company, and how I opened my home to host his out-of-town business associates and clients. Let me tell you how I accepted the news of a canceled family vacation with understanding each time he had a work emergency that took priority. And let me tell you how I did all this with grace and aplomb and without letting them see me sweat."

Now. Wouldn't you want this fierce warrior on your team?

You Can Do It

See your position through a new lens. You have more to offer than you realize.

I have a friend who worked on Wall Street and then reinvented herself as a project manager after nearly a dozen years away from the paid workforce. While she had never formally been a project manager before her career break, she knew that the skills she utilized as a busy mom of three and volunteer PTA president were transferable to the corporate arena.

She saw that she was a highly organized individual, an active listener, and one who was able to build consensus in the room. She knew how to get things done. And she knew that these were skills that were desirable in the workplace, too. And they are. If you're worried about translating your mom skills to a résumé, have a look at the sample supplied at the back of the book to help you get started. Note how results-oriented it is. This show-me-don't-just-tell-me approach, by the way, is what a prospective employer really wants to see.

Even if you've never held an official job but find that you want, or need, to take on that challenge, put yourself out there. Knock on as many doors as you can. Comb through your network. It may take a forward-thinking employer to consider you, but they're out there. And even if a few dozen prospects turn you down, be grateful for the indirect blessing. You wouldn't want to work for them anyway. After all, only the highly astute employer understands that while you can teach a valuable skill, you can't teach a valuable trait.

A Fresh Start

Whether you're returning to the workforce, entering it for the first time, or changing your career path, be kind to yourself in the transition. Don't twist yourself into a pretzel to make your case. Work with what you have and present it in as optimistic a package as you can.

Be sure to take the right steps:

- *Get help from a professional.* If it's been years since you've prepared a résumé, consider getting the help of a human resources professional. Not only will they know what key words to use and how to format it for a contemporary look, they'll know how to frame you to look your best. They'll give you the makeover you need. To make the process effective, however, gather all your relevant data ahead of time. And even if this is not your first rodeo, consider consulting with a professional anyway, particularly if you're switching fields.

- *Provide volunteer information.* This includes all volunteer work. Our skills and responsibilities are no less important or impactful just because we've not been paid for them. And if there's a volunteer position you can take on that might make you more attractive to a prospective employer, go ahead and grab it. As suggested in the chapter on exposure, this is a great way to get your toe in the water as you steer your life in a new direction.

- *Get certified.* Nothing freshens up your look like a certification course or two. Even if it's in something relatively simple or esoteric, the effort alone shows that you're engaged, interested in progress or change, capable of learning new skills, and willing to exercise some mental muscle. Best of all, it increases your credibility.

- *Lose the baggage.* This is your chance at a fresh start. At these pivotal points, leave the negatives behind and take with you only that which is positive, fulfilling, gratifying, healthy, inspiring, and useful. Decide what you don't want and what you do. Adopt a truly forward-looking approach. This is your moment to take the stage and shine.

Beginning with You

Be cognizant of the fact that we are social creatures who react to the visual. We can't help but notice each other, not to judge (although that happens, too) but simply to form an impression. Even before the advent of social media, this was always the case. Think about it. The only difference between our world and that of our grandmothers is that while they may have had only their town or village as their audience, we now have the potential for a much wider one.

Otherwise, human nature has remained fundamentally unchanged. People take in what we do, what we wear, how we work, how we play, what we say, and how we say it, even down to the words we choose. They look at how we react to certain situations, what we find amusing, how we treat others, and how we treat ourselves—including our health. Even our gait and posture do their part to shape an opinion.

That's why it's important to be self-aware.

This is especially true in the working world. You've heard the age-old advice that you should always dress for the role you want to play. And it's true. While your work speaks for itself, you give yourself that competitive edge by confirming in your boss's mind that, yes, he or she can picture you performing in a leadership role. In her book *Act Like a Leader, Think Like a Leader*, Herminia Ibarra (my girl crush) reinforces this concept and talks about acting like it before feeling like it. And even when we do become the person we want to be, we're not always going to feel 100 percent confident and comfortable. That's OK. It happens to all of us. With a little help, you'll learn how to put your best self forward even then.

By taking control of your brand, you control the image you cast. Remember this at all times. Think of what this means in the context of not just your close family and friends (even your significant other) but strangers, too.

Not long ago, I ran into an old acquaintance. After catching up on how we were each doing, she brought up the last time she had seen me, which was back in 1993. With a warm smile, she recalled the striking figure I had cut that day in my favorite power suit. It was—you guessed it—red. While this may be a superficial example about a fleeting moment, the image of me radiating confidence in a killer outfit was powerful enough to live in this person's memory for some twenty-odd years.

What about you? What impressions have you left along the way? Would you remember you? Would you like to change your image or improve it in some way? How do you want to reinvent yourself? How do you want others to see you?

Whatever your wish, you can make it happen by taking action. Remember, you're in control. It may take time—maybe longer than you like. Or it could happen overnight. It may take some strategic steps, but the tools are there.

Reach for them. Have faith. Be patient. And go for it.

12

TAKING STOCK

("Am I doing enough? Could I be doing more?")

In chapter 2 we asked ourselves, "Who am I?" Now that we've looked at the bigger picture, it's time to shift gears to a more pragmatic approach. This time, we ask, "*What* am I?"

This is where you go narrow and deep. This is where you make detailed lists of the strengths, weaknesses, skills, experiences, and abilities you've acquired or grown over the years. Now you're looking objectively at what you bring to the table. You're taking stock of what you have to offer a prospective employer and figuring out how best to leverage the unique package that you are. This is where you strut down that fashion runway of life and show the world whatcha got.

Digging for Your Gold

You may be wondering whether or not this is akin to building your résumé. The answer is yes, somewhat. And without a doubt, this is an exercise we should all do over the course of our lives. But for the more mature candidate, however, particularly one reinventing herself or trying to establish herself for the first time, this goes beyond the traditional résumé. The process of taking stock is what is needed to draw out those not-so-obvious strengths and weaknesses on which she can, and should, capitalize.

To take stock means several things: to make an inventory list; to make a general appraisal, especially of prospects and resources; to attach importance to; to think carefully about a situation or event and form an opinion about it.

The term "taking stock" likely has roots in commerce, where it literally meant recording what is in your inventory. As individuals, we may not count the number of widgets on our shelves. To be successful, however, each of us needs to keep a close and watchful eye on our own inventory and how it defines us.

Whether we are conscious of it or not, we are all walking and talking stockrooms. Each of us is as unique as the day unfolding right now. Our personal shelves are filled with everything that makes us who we are:

- Biases

- Education

- Experiences

- Fears

- Gaps

- Personality traits

- Shortcomings

- Skills

- Talents

- Upbringing

- Values

Just imagine the endless combinations.

What does your inventory look like? Is it heavy in one area and light in another? Has it changed over the years or remained stagnant? Do you see any obvious advantages to your list given your current situation?

This is data mining at its best because it's all about you. Make a habit of taking stock of yourself regularly. Discipline yourself to make it an annual or biannual exercise. Keep your notes stored away for future reference. As you grow older and evolve, as surely you will if you're the kind who's always sowing the seeds of progress, this exercise will inform the course your life is taking.

Advice from a List Lover

Taking stock naturally entails (surprise!) making lists that dig deep into all things *you*. Have fun by coming up with all sorts of categories, from the basic—like a "Strengths and Gaps" list—to the more private—like "Social Experiences." You want to ask yourself questions like:

- What am I good at? What am I not good at?

- What makes me relax? What gets my neck in a knot?

- What type of work would I refuse to do no matter how much it paid?

- What type of work would I do, or continue to do, even if I became a millionaire?

Beyond that, I recommend making aspirational lists, such as the attributes of "My Perfect Job" along with a "Can't Tolerate" list.

My Perfect Job	Can't Tolerate
People oriented	Blatant dishonesty and deception
Environment that values learning	Hostile or toxic work culture
Role with a business impact	Lack of accountability
Boss who is invested in my success	Incompetence
Freedom to be creative	Lack of managerial courage
Relationships matter	Indecisiveness

Always remember that you are more than what you know. I was a finance major in college. But just because I switched fields, it doesn't mean that the knowledge went to waste or was no longer a marketable skill. Rather, I took from that finance major a deep understanding and appreciation for how businesses function and added to it a framework that I've applied in every role I've ever had.

Collecting and Connecting

We've established the fact that you're this beautiful puzzle with all the pieces scattered on a table. But in order to complete the whole *you*, you must collect the pieces and determine how best to connect them to your work and personal lives. The success of this exercise rests on the quality of effort you put into it. Be detailed. Take your time. Enjoy the process. Slowly, the picture will take shape.

Look inside for your own themes, not only at work but in your personal life:

- What were or are your favorite things to do outside of school or work?

- Why do you think those extracurricular activities add a shine to your cheek?

- How can you infuse that connectedness into your current career? What about a new one?

Take the example of the individual who seems to be the go-to person for advice. Are colleagues constantly seeking your counsel on office politics? Do your friends often come to you for parenting or relationship tips? Do they see you as someone with killer time-management skills? Are colleagues and friends always asking you to read anything they've written? Or are you the beauty-tips person? What about restaurant suggestions? Do friends think you're a foodie at large?

Ask yourself the following:

- Why is that?

- What draws people to me?

- What qualities in me make this logical?

With some introspection, you may discover some really cool things about yourself:

- Others find you approachable.

- You reflect back to people with kindness.

- People generally consider you trustworthy.

- You have a way of seeing all sides of a situation.

- You have perspective from your own experiences.

- Your honest and generous feedback is usually constructive.

- You have the ability to make people feel heard and validated.

- Your knowledge level in your area of expertise is higher than you knew.

- Your natural empathic nature enables you to connect with others in a way that is comforting and useful.

It's also a useful exercise to think about the reason you excel at these things:

- You have endless patience because you have young children or grew up with pets.

- You're a good leader because you're the oldest one in the family.

- You're naturally diplomatic because you have been exposed to conflict.

- You're comfortable with budgeting because you put yourself through college.

- You gravitate to teaching because you had a friend or sibling who struggled in school and helped them with their homework.

- You're a good listener because you grew up in a large family where someone was always seeking your advice or talking.

Resolve to leverage your talents regardless of whether that skill set came from a classroom or from life. Be deliberate about this. Put those mental muscles to work. If you don't, your raw talents and strengths will only atrophy into limp limbs. I have always had a passion for interior decorating, something I know I have an eye for. Even though it has nothing to do with my current career, I may just one day take a walk down that path if, or when, the time is right.

Know It So You Can Show It

Some folks are extremely self-aware when it comes to their capabilities and strong suits. You've met these exceptional individuals. They're the ones who seem to hold their chin up just a bit higher. They're not easily deterred by a no, thwarted by a setback, or distracted by a passing fancy. When you leave their company, you sense immediately that you were in the presence of someone who has their stuff together.

Most people are not as tuned in. They are the ones who find it difficult to identify their strengths, much less articulate them. They appear to have no real center. If you think you might be in the latter category, seek the help of tools such as the book *StrengthsFinder 2.0* by Tom Rath. These incredible to-the-point and at-your-fingertips resources can help to narrow and quantify your strengths while providing context around how they can be deployed. With this deeper understanding of what you bring to the table, you will join the first group with confidence.

Drill deep.

Identify patterns.

Know what motivates you.

Take note of what you can get lost in for hours. Once that's done, make it your side job to watch for opportunities to take it to another level. In other words, seek your calling. I did just that when I formed my consultancy company and named it after my passion for helping people find theirs: SYNC—Seek Your Natural Calling.

Weakness or Fear Factor?

But what about those areas where our star shines a little—or a lot—less brightly? Where we don't feel 100 percent strong.

While the same process of taking stock applies, the action items may be different. No one is advocating that you take on a profession that makes you yawn or look incompetent unless you're deliberately seeking to overcome a weak area as a personal challenge.

That said, what you perceive as a weakness or gap may be nothing more than something you haven't yet explored—quite possibly out of fear of failure. But it is these overlooked paths and tunnels that could potentially lead to enormous treasures.

Some of us find our voice only by going outside our comfort zone. Taking a position outside of the United States was both one of the scariest and most rewarding parts of my career. But not only did I gain an understanding about how business is conducted outside the United States, I also learned a lot about myself and competencies I never knew I had.

Are You Bad at It or Just Unfamiliar with It?

Similarly, once you identify gaps, you may find that they are easier to address than you thought. If you lack technical skills—say, using Excel, for example—find a class and take it. Avail yourself of development opportunities through your employer, online classes—many of which are free these days through massive open online courses (MOOC)—or even YouTube videos.

You may discover that you still have neither love nor knack for it, and that's quite all right. In fact, it can be a great relief to confirm what's definitely off the table. Just don't confuse being unfamiliar with something with being bad at it.

Begin Investing Now

If you're young and just beginning your career adventure, you may feel you have little to say about yourself. Don't sweat it. Just get used to the feel of self-auditing. Even a couple of basic observations will do. Before you know it, you will have mastered this important leadership skill that will set you apart from your peers.

Remember: *self-awareness is your secret weapon.*

On the flip side, it's never too late to begin investing in yourself. If you're past the grasshopper stage, have serious fun with your stock-taking exercise. It may just be one of the kindest things you do for yourself. After all, you've lived a little and seen some battles in your time. You've got a lot to say—more than you realize. Celebrate that.

Make this investment of time on an ongoing basis as your portfolio changes over the years. Treasure it. Look at it often. Be strategic in what you add to it. Congratulate yourself for any increment of growth—progress is a plus no matter how small. Choose wisely how to spend your energy toward building your portfolio, and you'll have the gift of a fulfilling life.

Once you've seen yourself in your truest form—without the filters or high-angle shots—and once you've sketched out your future's blueprint, you're ready to take that first step out into the world or make a fresh start toward a brand-new destination.

13

CREATING YOUR SUCCESS TOOLKIT

("Sometimes I feel as if I've gone
camping without the right gear.")

You may be asking what all this means. Why should you care about what the pages in these past twelve chapters had to say?

In a 2013 Harris survey for the University of Phoenix, researchers found that "nearly 80 percent of workers in their 20s said they wanted to change careers, followed by 64 percent of 30-somethings and 54 percent in their 40s.. It went on to say that, "although the majority of workers in this survey said they had had career plans when they were younger, 73 percent of them had not yet landed in the job they had expected. That's almost three-quarters of those in the study. Indeed, only 14 percent of those surveyed said they held their "dream job." But that's not all. The survey also found that women were more likely than men to be in a different job than they had anticipated.

These figures should make you feel a small panic rising in your gut.

This is not a statistic about job satisfaction. It's really about happiness. And these numbers don't exactly paint a happy picture.

In case you're too young to fully appreciate what this feels like over the course of one decade, let alone several, let's make it more personal.

I want you to imagine your least favorite chore. The one that makes your shoulders drop when you're asked to do it. Yes—that one. Now I want you to picture doing this five days a week for eight to ten hours a day for an entire month. Then multiply that for as many months as you think you can stand it.

"Ugh" is right. And if you're tempted to argue that money would be compensation enough for a job that drains you of joy or purpose, let me save you the inevitable heartache and money spent at the therapist's. While money and all its trappings can make you feel accomplished, it won't feed your soul. You'll only end up using that money to medicate yourself at the mall.

Planning for It

Let's go back for a moment to that statistic about the 73 percent who missed their target despite having plans. While we can only speculate why this is so, it is my hope that you won't be among them. That is the reason for this guide.

More importantly, I hope you're beginning to see how dangerously easy it is to slip through those proverbial cracks. Those of us who can count our age in decades know this from either personal experience or close observation. What we are telling you, our dear younger sisters, is that this all too common story usually comes about not because of a single sensational event but rather because of a lack of discipline. Apathy can have a lingering and unpleasant aftertaste. Don't be that girl. Don't have others telling your story and ending it with "What a waste."

Perhaps you've heard it said before that no one actually wakes up one morning and decides that this will be the day they deep-six their future. Well, it's true. The process is much more insidious.

An underwhelming ending usually begins with a series of innocuous missteps that often go unnoticed and unchecked. On their own they mean nothing—"no biggie," as we like to say. String them together, however, and the pattern becomes clear. Before you know it you have a destructive habit in the making and an avoidable disappointment in the offing. Do you see yourself or anyone you know in this list?

- Alarm habitually is not set. Your fingers can find the snooze button with your eyes closed.

- Classes are skipped repeatedly. Assignments are rushed, only partially done, or not submitted at all.

- Test scores come in lower than needed. Scholarship hopes go from high to hazy.

- Appointments are missed, whether personal or work related.

- Follow-up calls or emails are not made or are done too late to be effective.

- Thank-you messages are not sent on time or at all.

- Deadlines are grazed or botched.

- Promises are not kept, whether to coworkers, superiors, family, or friends. A bad reputation takes root.

- Résumés are written in a rush and not even proofread.

- Opportunities are not explored, calculated risks not taken.

- Bills are paid late, interest accrues, and your credit score pays the price.

- Over-the-top spending becomes the norm.

- Networking is not done. Research and information gathering is weak at best.

Would you ever be as blasé about your next vacation? I doubt it. You'd immediately hit all the travel sites, social media, and friends for anything you can find out about your destination. You'd make lists of landmarks to see, transportation choices available, and restaurants to explore. And let's not get started on the hotel. Without even being told to, you're already checking out the gym facilities, Wi-Fi options, pull-out couch availability, bed linen quality, and more, weeks or even months before you're due to arrive.

And yet so many people give much less thought to planning their future. I've said before that life can, and will, throw you some unexpected surprises. Not all of them good, either. It will demand faith and agility on your part. But I still argue that if you make your plans and put actual substance behind them (i.e., do more than just wishing them into existence), you'll get there.

OK, I'm Sold. What Should I Pack?

In the last twelve chapters, we talked about many of the ingredients to success. Now it's time to put all of these pieces together and create what I like to call your success toolkit. And I mean a literal collection of go-to items that you can reach for just as you would a toolbox with which to make home repairs. It can take any form that's comfortable for you:

- A digital folder

- A paper folder

- A simple box

- A scrapbook

- Anything you like

This is your personal arsenal.

Make it as spectacular or simple as you want. Look at it not as the answer to every question you may have but as a compendium of resources you find valuable, whether for concrete information or general encouragement that resonates with you.

Perhaps you want to keep the first job rejection letters you ever got out of college as a reminder that "no" doesn't mean "never." Maybe you want to keep a collection of positive Instagram reviews received on the paintings you did in your weekend art class. What about a list of publishing agents representing authors who write in the genre you're interested in?

Anything goes as long as it acts like a treasure trove of tips for you. When you turn to your toolkit, it needs to advance your narrative in some way.

My kit includes the following:

- A list of people I follow on Twitter, LinkedIn, and more

- Apps that make my life easier in general

- Biographies and how-to books that motivate me

- Mastermind group contacts I have met and groups I want to join

- Names of friends and acquaintances, along with their professions, skills, or industry affiliations

- Networking groups in my field that ensure that I stay abreast of news, conferences, and the latest commentary from industry leaders

- Relevant RSS feeds I subscribe to that are relevant to my field

What will you collect for your kit? Have fun with it, not just in terms of what you gather but how you arrange it. Pool together everything that helps you put your best foot forward. In addition to the tools we've discussed throughout this book (i.e., your lists of goals, accomplishments, charts outlining your strengths and weaknesses, likes and dislikes, and so forth), you could add some or all of the following:

- Your updated résumé, so that it's ready to be sent off at a moment's notice

- Sample request letters (e.g. for a meeting, opportunity to pitch an idea, etc.)

- Sample thank-you letters or notes for different occasions that strike different tones (e.g. formal, business casual, etc.)

- Up-to-date professional headshots

- Headhunting firms, career counselors, or similar contacts

- Various pithy bios or profiles about yourself to enhance your social media presence

- Memorable conversation openers to use when meeting strangers at an event (yes, really—conversation is an art form)

- List of personal hacks to calm and center yourself when you're in public or about to give a presentation

- Reminders of awesome out-of-character things you did, like entering a dance competition at a holiday resort

- Reminders of personal feats of bravery, such as confronting a friend or colleague who had crossed the line in some way

- Your gym workout routine (weights and reps) when in your best shape ever or best times when at the peak of your marathon training

Using your toolkit, you should be able to do the following:

- Articulate your strengths, capabilities, knowledge, and transferable skills through your updated résumés and stocktaking exercises

- Follow up quickly on any opportunities that come your way

- Identify mentors, champions, and allies

- Offer links to your own web presence (e.g., blogs and social media accounts)

- Recognize those areas that you want to develop further and programs or people that can help you achieve this

- Share your personal stories that reflect who you are, what you're made of, and what you bring to the table

- Understand which environments play to your strengths and why

More than Just Friends

Because your friends can be a valuable source of information and networking, they are a part of your success.

Yet how many of us consider reaching out for their insights on the challenges experienced and opportunities offered in their respective fields? And if you're still too young to have working friends, what about their parents or older siblings? Could they be a helpful source of information or contacts? If you view these individuals as possible gatekeepers to different arenas orbiting your world, then you'll see what a rich network you actually have, even if you're still in college.

As a general rule, therefore, it would be wise to keep the channels of communication open instead of waiting until you need a favor, an introduction, or information. While some may be good-natured about it, others may feel that they are being used.

Be proactive. Keep the channels of communication current. Strike up a conversation. Ask thought-provoking questions (e.g., "What would surprise people the most about your profession if they were to learn about it?"). Show genuine interest. Follow up on past conversations (e.g., "That presentation you were preparing for when we spoke a month ago, how did it go?").

Do this and you could be creating a path to a possible internship or job.

No Excuse

While it's axiomatic that technology has made life easier in general for us all, it is equally true that it has shut the door on laziness and excuses when it comes to arming yourself with information.

With companies maintaining vast social media profiles, there is simply no excuse for not doing your homework on prospective employers that interest you. Use the wondrous tool that is the Internet to your advantage. If you want to work for Company X, comb through its web presence and go even beyond its public site to its social media presence. In many cases, social media platforms are used for job postings rather than the more traditional job sites.

And should you be fortunate enough to gain an interview at your desired company, know that you will be expected to arrive at that privileged meeting with a deep knowledge of its business model, clients, and culture. The bar is now higher than ever. As we move into the future, there will be fewer excuses to utter the words, "I don't know" or "I didn't know that."

Being Ready to Pounce

Presenting yourself to the world is a job in itself.

Preparing your toolkit is also no small task—especially at the beginning. But do the work and it'll pay off beautifully. This level of comprehensive groundwork makes you more nimble when faced with opportunities that spring up unexpectedly, as many life-changing opportunities do. And success belongs to those ready to pounce on an opportunity they don't see coming.

Let's say, for instance, that you and I are meeting each other for the first time at a wedding reception. Your engaging personality and sharp wit come shining through as we help ourselves to wine and hors d'oeuvres. At the end of our robust chat, I say that I'm quite impressed with what I've heard and would love to see your résumé. You smile because I've just given you my business card and you now know that I am a seasoned human resources professional with a rich and diverse network to share. You can't believe your lucky break. As we shake hands, signaling the end of the conversation, I add quickly, "Really great meeting you! I'll look out for your email Monday morning, then. Can't wait to see it."

Are you still smiling? Would you be able to send it to me by 9:00 a.m.? Or are you now silently panicking?

Don't expect your toolkit to be a bag of tricks. Rather, much like the carry-on bag you fly with, your toolkit should contain a small subset of the critical things you need close to you at all times to ensure that you're always comfortably situated. This is how you equip your way to success. This is what moves you to the next leg of the journey.

And remember, perhaps the most important thing to include in your toolkit is an open mind. Be open to opportunities outside of your comfort zone, and be open to qualities that others see in you. Sometimes, you might just surprise yourself.

LAST THOUGHTS

("Ahh. *There* she is.")

The morning the Twin Towers took their final bow, I was in my car, midspan on the George Washington Bridge. As my office at J.P. Morgan was a mere block and a half away from the World Trade Center, my routine was to take the train in from my New Jersey home into Manhattan. Had I done that on this particular morning, I would have already been at my office the moment the first plane hit, most likely working on my second cup of coffee while admiring the crystal blue sky that New York had woken up to that fateful day. But because I had an after-work function to attend later that evening, I drove instead.

When the traffic stopped abruptly as I was crossing the bridge, I thought nothing of it at first. This was New York. Traffic happens. But after some fifteen minutes had passed, I switched on the radio to see what was happening. That was the moment I stepped through a portal into a parallel world. Suddenly, I heard familiar voices that no longer sounded like themselves. Local radio personalities who once waxed suave with their slick radio voices were now almost struggling to get their words out. Over and over I heard them saying, "World Trade Center!"

I whipped my head to the right. There in the distance, like a scene out of a high-end Hollywood action film, were the landmark towers, engulfed in flames and smoke.

It took me about ten full seconds to accept that what I was seeing was real. And when I finally did, my body began to tremble uncontrollably as the horror unfolded before me. When the cars finally began to inch forward, I pulled over once I was safely on the New York side. I had to get my heart to stop racing before I could continue driving. Forty-five minutes later, I finally turned on the ignition and began snaking my way back home to New Jersey through Westchester at twenty miles per hour. When I got home almost six hours later, at three o'clock that afternoon, I learned that authorities had actually shut down the George Washington Bridge, thinking that it was another potential target.

In the moments and months that followed, unfiltered emotions flooded every cell in my body as certain messages suddenly zoomed into focus. First among them was the importance of my family and loved ones. If I hadn't known before how much I needed them, I knew it now. I showered them with more love and appreciation than I'd known I had. The feeling of making sure we stayed together—whether through get-togethers or phone calls—hit me with a sense of urgency.

But one message shot to the forefront of my mind and never left: *Lisa, you really don't have all the time in the world as you thought you did. And God didn't put you here to waste the precious talent He blessed you with. So get on it.*

Don't die with the dream inside you.

Don't give up on yourself, ever.

Each time you lose, you learn. If you're not losing now and then, you're probably not taking chances. When you fall, get up, dust yourself off, try again, and feel proud of yourself for finding the courage to get into that ring. So many never do. More importantly, don't give up on yourself by giving away your power and placing your future entirely in the hands of one person. They may have the best of intentions, but they shouldn't be the one to control your life.

Earlier usually makes it easier, but at some point you must make a plan YOU. Make yourself the focus of your blueprint. And while you're at it, think of your backup plan, too.

Do the work. Wake up each morning, acknowledge that you've just been given the gift of a new day, and stand guard against the three *Is*:

1. *Indecision.* Each time you neglect to make a decision on something, you're giving up your right to control your life. Even if it turns out to be the wrong decision, you'll feel empowered for having called the shots. Set goals. Make your choices. Take action.

2. *Inertia.* Just as your body will wither in the absence of motion, so will that beautiful mind of yours. Learn. Try. Do. Explore the computer that is your brain. It has more genius apps than you'll ever know.

3. *Insipidity.* Let enthusiasm sit in your passenger seat however you live and work. Express your joy as only you would. What may show on the outside for some as a loud "Woo-hoo!" may appear as a quiet "Ahh" in the eyes for another. Either way, open wide and really taste life.

These three *I*'s are your life's enemies. Nothing breeds discontent more than they do.

If Wishes Were Horses

I said at the start of this journey that, in many ways, this book is my note to my younger self. It is a personal offering I hope you will benefit from. But before I dismount, I'd like to give you one final assignment.

I would like you to write a letter to your future self. It doesn't matter how old you are, and it doesn't have to include a list of things you'll own, be, or do. Rather, you can simply tell yourself how proud you are of the confident, independent-thinking woman you will become in the future, and how proud you are that you took the steps necessary to put that crown on every day and keep it there. And thank yourself for remembering that it took work to achieve this, not just wishes.

That said, I want to remind you that the work does, in fact, begin inside us with our very thoughts. It is the reason why so many versions of the following quote exist, going all the way back to the Bible and ancient Chinese philosophers. Of all the quotes I keep close by, it is my favorite:

Watch your thoughts;
They become words.
Watch your words;
They become actions.
Watch your actions;
They become habits.
Watch your habits;
They become character.
Watch your character;
It becomes your destiny.

I would also like to take an indulgent moment to include a final summary of some of the takeaways I want to leave you with and a few personal "always and never" rules. While I live by these, I am the first to admit that I still have to work at some of them.

Take from the list what you will and add your own:

- *Always challenge what you read or what you hear.* Do this not to be difficult but to train yourself to think for yourself. I expect this even from my own students. I am but one person with one perspective. I want to hear their take on something I've shared. Challenge even those beliefs you've held for as long as you've known yourself. Nothing is more empowering than to say sincerely, "You know, I never thought about it that way", or "I see it differently now", or "Yes, I can see that things have changed."

- *Never stop learning, even when you've left the classroom.* Promise yourself that you'll make an effort to learn anything, from knitting to salsa dancing to cooking to gardening, as long as it gets your neurons going. Learn a second language, if even just conversationally. In the United States, only 8 percent of those whose first language is English can communicate with someone in a foreign language.

- *Always find ways to give back.* Whether you see it or not, you got to where you are with some help. Become a mentor to an underprivileged child or one with overwhelmed parents (or parent). Carve out some time for public service when you can. Join a charity or community club that supports the underserved of society. It will keep you grounded in ways that cutting a check sometimes cannot. And if you can't fit that in, then lift someone's spirits with a kind word, smile, or gesture as you go through your day. You never know what kind of awful day they may be having.

- *Always treasure your health, from mental to spiritual to physical.* The body may extend you generous credit terms while you're still young and strong. But it will surely keep a running tab on your choices. If you indulge unabatedly in dangerous or questionable behavior in any or all three areas, you will eventually get the bill.

- *Never burn your bridges.* These sage words of advice could not be truer with the advent of social media. With technology's expansion shrinking the world, we are more connected than ever before. I am not suggesting that you choke on your truth. Instead, I'm suggesting that you express it in a way that does not shut down opportunities—including opportunities for forgiveness.

- *Never nurse old wounds.* While this is probably one of the hardest things to do, especially when an issue remains unresolved, I don't know of anyone who can hold a grudge without looking unattractive and bitter. You don't want to be that person. You have better things to do than to waste time on something that will only hurt you more and sap you of precious energy.

- *Always remember that there is grace in gratitude.* I still catch myself disappearing down the worry well when one corner of my life gets swept up in a mini tornado. But when I do, I stop to close my eyes, breathe deeply, and thank God for even the simplest of blessings He has given me. And I remind myself that no matter how bad I think I have it, there is someone out there who would swap their bag of problems for mine in a heartbeat.

- *Always keep an appetite for calculated risks while you can still handle the heartburn.* Step outside of your comfort zone. Most hugely successful people don't coast their way to glory. They work and fight for every ounce of it. Overnight success rarely sticks, anyway. If that were true, lottery winners would remain wealthy for the rest of their lives. So if you're seeing hammocks suddenly appearing in your life, run.

- *Always, but always, play to your superpowers.* Really delve into your natural-born gifts. They are indeed gifts from God. Treasure them. Use them wisely. If you spend a third of your waking hours working, you won't find joy doing something that produces average results at best. Find ways to make your talents work for you, even if you have to get help to make this possible. Ask. Negotiate. Never sit there assuming that the answer will be no.

- Finally, *always live by your highest standards, even when there's no one around to see, whether it's at work or in your personal life.* This includes how you treat yourself, even in the thoughts you think and the words you say. You will sleep better not just for having made the right choices but also for knowing that you honored yourself by doing your best.

And now for a few "I hope's" as together we continue the movement to rewrite the narrative for today's woman:

- I hope that gone are the days when our sisters, nieces, and daughters bought into the belief that ambition is a marriage's natural enemy. If your significant other is intimidated by your personal drive and long-term career goals, you have to ask yourself whether you're in the right relationship. And if you take on the role of imposter to accommodate your relationship, you likely won't be able to stay very long. Neither of you will be happy.

- I hope the playbook of the future includes entire scenes where the switching of gender roles, whether out of necessity or choice, no longer elicits curious glances or surprised smiles. I would, therefore, be remiss if I ended this book without tipping my hat to the phenomenal men out there who have stepped into the role of primary caregiver. Once an urban myth, these progressive men are helping to make change possible. For this reason they, too, are pioneers in their own right. After all, let us not forget that societal pressures swing both ways. I'm sure many men can share stories of double glances sent their way while they were walking around with a diaper bag hanging from their shoulder.

- And I hope the playbook of the future includes detailed examples of trendsetting corporations, like Zoetis, that changed the rules and attitudes so that women stepping into the arena could have a fair shot at winning. This will also mean taking the courageous step of making structural adjustments in the area of childcare, whether it's in the form of maternity leave, onsite or offsite day care, or technology such as nanny cams. However we get there, we must work to welcome the day when a mother working outside the home does not feel immediately pinned against a wall when her child becomes ill or a meeting goes on longer than planned and it's now past dinnertime.

Who's That Lady?

Over the years, I've sometimes thought about the day I saw that striking woman, now almost thirty-five years ago.

Even though she never looked my way, the image of her going past my mom and me remained fixed in my memory like an old photo in a keepsake box. I'd like to think that she was destined to walk by us at that moment and imprint on my young mind. I didn't have the words to express it at the time, but I knew instinctively that I wanted to feel the way she looked. I wanted that aura—the one that said that this was a woman who knew herself and who was both actor and director in the story of her life.

During the course of writing this book, I thought of her more often and wondered how her life unfolded after that day. What did she do with her talents? What dreams did she conquer? How many checkmarks did she have on her list? Did she have any disappointments? How did she work through them? What about regrets? And what messages would she share with us if she could?

My mystery lady would be in her early seventies today. I wish I could tell her that she played a part in helping to shape a young woman's life, if even in a small way. I wish I could show her *my* confident stride and tell her about the journey that led me to find it.

It is my wish that you will be that woman someday.

You'll be the one going about your day, unaware that you've just won the attention of a wide-eyed young woman a generation or two behind you. She may even be an impressionable little girl still holding her mother's hand as she stops to stare and ask who you are. She won't be able to explain why she can't stop looking. She won't have the words. But she will know that, one day, she, too, will walk the way you do, with your shoulders pulled back, your chin tilted up, and your eyes fierce with contentment.

Sample Résumé

Any Woman

123 Anywhere Road   555.555.5555

Any City, Any State, Zip   email address

LEADERSHIP PROFILE & CAREER HIGHLIGHTS

A highly motivated individual with strong consultative, sales and negotiating skills and proven record of achievement in high-profile service/product sectors. Possess the ability to function successfully in a variety of environments and cultures. Experience includes, but is not limited to, the following:

Sales Management Revenue Generation Relationship Development

- Innovative Leadership
- Telecommunications
- Client Satisfaction
- Sales Direction
- Campaign Formulation
- Staff Development
- Business/ Sales Development
- Goal Attainment
- Strategic Marketing
- Project Management
- Strategic Planning
- Competitive Analysis

SKILLS

Strategic Planning	Financial Planning	Change Leader
Conflict Resolution	SpecialistInnovator	Logistics
Coordination		

EXPERIENCE

PTA President, Our Town, Middle School, USA

Responsible for development, growth, and management of school programs. Established relationships with new and prospective parents and informed them about various after-school programs and educational efforts to increase positive student experiences. Created and implemented new testing solutions to increase college entrance. Collaborated with various local entities to enhance the parent-teacher-school relationship. Guided a team of 5 volunteer aides.

- Promoted cross-functional work teams within the school, which resulted in enhanced coordination of projects and decreased waste.

- Increased overall membership by 15% by cultivating strong relationships with existing members and utilizing a proactive approach to bring new parents into the organization.

- Developed and conducted the first mentoring seminar for the middle school, which led to a 12% increase in achievement test scores.

- Promoted LEED-certified building renovations.

United Way, Associate, Our Town, USA

Increased local volunteer rate by 10% by reinforcing alliances with existing partners and building new relationships with local businesses.

- Managed local blood drives and provided follow-up information and status reports to participating organizations. This led to increased participation from alliances.

- Communication point person for community outreach efforts. Ensured events were promoted and encouraged attendance. These efforts ensured events were highly populated.

- Served as community liaison for fundraising. Leveraged previous business contacts.

PROFESSIONAL ACCOMPLISHMENTS

- Recognized as Volunteer of the Year – 2017 by United Way, Bergen County, NJ
- Raised $100,000 for back-to-school supplies
- Raised $200,000 for local women's shelter

| **EDUCATION** | **B.B.A., Yorkshire Pudding University,** East West, NJ |
| **REFERENCES** | Furnished upon request |

ACKNOWLEDGMENTS

No labor of love is ever possible without the encouragement and support from family and friends, not to mention the occasional cracking of the whip. And this endeavor is no exception.

I am especially indebted to my editor, Alexandra Lee, for her exceptional ability to coax out of her authors the most authentic material locked deep inside them. Because of you, Alex, I was able to produce the hardest chapters of this book—the ones I didn't want to write because I feared they would expose my soul. Not only did you help me to improve the book's structure and focus, but you also showed me how to frame my missteps, successes, and all the wonderful adventures in between within the context of my overarching message. Your project management skills, encouragement, and validation of my stories have been a Godsend. Thank you.

Judy DiClemente, you have no idea how much of a blessing you have been to me in this process. It was your strong voice of practicality and gentle encouragement that kickstarted this journey years ago. Thank you for testing my theories with your amazing daughters. You, my dear, are gifted. Your daughters are a testament of that.

Bridgitt Haarsgaard, you are one of the most generous people I know. I often refer to you as my "Google Friend" because there isn't anything you don't know or anyone you're not connected to. Thank you for your steadfast encouragement and partnership. It means more than you could ever know.

Kim Greaux and Lamarda Brooks, my two sisters-in-law. I thank God for you both. In fact, forget the in-law part. You are my sisters, period. You encouraged me to write my story for the next generation of women leaders. I'm so glad my brother and I had the good sense to marry well.

To Mildred Greaux, my mother-in-law. Millie (that's what we call you affectionately behind your back), you are an amazing woman and feisty warrior. Who else but you would be cutting down the trees in her backyard at the ripe old age of eighty-five and calling people to task? (You go, girl!) Ma, you have always believed in me. I will forever be grateful for your love, generosity of spirit, and encouragement.

To my young nieces, Chauryce, Shay, Jasmine, Nakima, and Elon, you know I think there's nothing you can't do. I hope that you use this book as a guide, a blueprint, and a roadmap so that your road may be a little less bumpy. Your horizon is filled with endless possibilities, and it is my wish that you pursue them with courage and curiosity. I'm so proud of you and stand in awe of you. Shine on, brilliant, bold, and beautiful women. #Girlboss.

To my personal village. You never hesitate to pull me back to reality when I have ventured too far off course. You are my faithful sounding board. You reframe my worldview when my windshield needs defrosting. So, to Dr. Denise Williams, Pierre Dobson, and Michele Phillips, thank you-all for your endless wisdom, support, and sense of humor as you saw me through this project. May you never stop breaking out into the happy dance at a moment's notice.

Gloria Basse, Sabina Gasper, and Rebecca Cisek. We spent countless hours strategizing on how to ensure our voices were heard in meetings. Thank you for being women who support other women. Far too often we hear of the opposite. Together, we prevailed and rewrote the script.

Yolanda DeJesus-Alicia and Nadia Richardson. I love that we began planning the book launch party before it was even finished. Thank you for always thinking of ways to celebrate the milestones and keeping me encouraged when the writing process was getting stale.

Stacey Apple and Marianne Strobel, we've been friends for decades and have been there for each other through thick and thin. You always loved the idea of a book and helped me see myself with the finished work in hand. Thank you for your never-ending support and for providing opportunities to showcase my work. (You know there isn't much I wouldn't do for a good bottle of wine or a Snickers bar.)

For your endless support and love, thank you to dear friends and colleagues Dr. Sandra Palmer, Fie, Marji Najac, Lisa Mathis, Sandy Clare, Wendy Taccetta, and all my mentees. For allowing me to share your stories with my readers, thank you, Yolanda Barham, Nadia Richardson, and Noribel Martinez. To the best coaches and mentors anyone could want, thank you, Toby Tetenbaum and Clint Lewis for your constant support. To the Zoetis Women's Council, you guys rock! It was an honor to be your executive sponsor.

Joey. Even though you prefer Joe, I will always call you Joey, my dear brother. You always thought I had superpowers and could do anything I set my mind to. I was a little sister growing up in the shadows of her accomplished older brother and had the great fortune of watching him go out and conquer the world. So, naturally I thought I could, too. You were my example of dignity, faith, and humility. Thank you for paving the way for me.

To my husband, Carl. You are my blanket and my love. It's remarkable how you choose only to see the best in me, every day, even on my worst days. I love how you always think I look amazing, especially when I know it's one of "those" days. You, my dear, are that rare combination of strength and sensitivity, and I'm so proud that you are completely comfortable holding your own. Your feedback and input have been invaluable to this process, and your suggestions have made this book all the richer. I can still hear you saying, "Provide examples, Lisa." Thank you for the countless hours of listening to me obsess over a paragraph or sentence and acting as if it was the first time you were hearing it. Now that's love. I'm so blessed for having you in my life.

Finally, I give thanks and praise to God for this work and for ordering all the steps that led to its completion.

ABOUT THE AUTHOR

Lisa Brooks-Greaux, EdD., currently serves on the faculties of Montclair State University and Manhattanville College where she teaches in their respective MBA programs. Before becoming a consultant and an educator, she enjoyed a long and distinguished career as a sales and talent development executive, taking her own talent to multinational companies such as Pfizer Inc., Verizon Wireless, JP Morgan Chase, Zoetis, and Delphi, Inc. During her time at Verizon, she held three consecutive positions overseas in Greece, Indonesia, and the Czech Republic. A familiar voice on the speaking circuit, a prominent figure in the world of mentoring, and a tireless advocate for the advancement of women, diversity, and inclusion in the workplace, Lisa was recognized by *The Network Journal* in 2000 as one of the 25 Most Influential Black Women in Business. In 2012, she founded SYNC Worldwide, a company through which she works with individuals to develop their leadership abilities and with multiple Fortune 500 companies to address business imperatives in the context of talent and leadership. Most recently, in 2018, she received the Professing Excellence Award from Montclair State University. The author now lives in New Jersey with her husband.

Want to reach out to the author? Find and follow her on:

www.syncworldwide.com
instagram: s.y.n.c.seekyournaturalcalling

Bibliography

1. Babcock, Linda, and Sara Laschever. *Women Don't Ask.* Bantam Dell, 2007.

2. Brzezinski, Mika. *Know Your Value.* Weinstein Books, 2011.

3. Buckingham, Marcus. *Go Put Your Strengths to Work.* Free Press, 2007.

4. Frohlinger, Carol, J.D. *Her Place at the Table.* Jossey-Bass, 2010.

5. Goffee, Rob. *Why Should Anyone be Led by You?* Harvard Business Review Press, 2006.

6. Huffington, Arianna. *On Becoming Fearless.* Little, Brown and Company, 2006.

7. Ibarra, Herminia. *Act Like a Leader, Think Like a Leader.* Harvard Business Review Press, 2015.

8. Kay, Katty. *The Confidence Code.* HarperCollins, 2014.

9. Klaus, Peggy. *Brag.* Hachette Book Group, 2003.

10. Klauser, Henriette Anne. *Write it Down, Make it Happen.* Simon & Schuster, 2000.

11. Loehr, Jim. *The Power of Story.* The Free Press, 2007

12. Rath, Tom. *StrengthsFinder.* Gallup Press, 2007.

13. Sandberg, Sheryl. *Lean In.* Alfred A. Knopf, 2013.

Notes

[i] Linda Babcock, Sara Laschever, *Women Don't Ask* (New York: Bantam Books, 2007), 2.

[ii] Katty Kay, Claire Shipman, *The Confidence Code* (New York: HarperCollins Publishers, 2014), 22.

[iii] Joyce Ehrlinger et al, "Why People Fail to Recognize Their Own Incompetence," *Current Directions in Psychological Science,* no. 3 (2003), 86.

[iv] Kay, Shipman, *The Confidence Code*, 170.

[v] Andrew Goldman, "Katie Couric Has a Few Regrets," *The New York Times Magazine*, April 4, 2011, MM14.

[vi] Goldman, "Katie Couric Has a Few Regrets," MM14.

[vii] Webster's Dictionary for Students, "Power." Webster's Dictionary for Students. Merriam-Webster, Incorporated, 2011, 14th edition, 125.

[viii] Patricia Reaney, "Dream Job? Most U.S. Workers want to change careers – poll" (New York: Reuters, 2013), 186.

[ix] Reaney, "Dream Job? Most U.S. Workers Want to Change Careers – poll," 186.